# The New Testament Picture Bible

### SCRIPT BY IVA HOTH
### ILLUSTRATIONS BY ANDRE LE BLANC
### BIBLE EDITOR, C. ELVAN OLMSTEAD, PH. D.

CHARIOT BOOKS™
DAVID C. COOK PUBLISHING CO.

PUBLISHED BY DAVID C. COOK PUBLISHING CO., ELGIN, IL 60120

FIRST PRINTING, 1990.

95 94 93 92 91     10 9 8 7 6 5 4 3 2

ISBN: 1-55513-542-0

# The Life of Jesus

FROM MATTHEW, MARK, LUKE, AND JOHN

THE FIRST FOUR BOOKS OF THE NEW TESTAMENT ARE CALLED THE GOSPELS, WHICH MEANS "GOOD NEWS"--ABOUT JESUS: HIS LIFE, TEACHINGS, DEATH, AND RESURRECTION. BECAUSE THE BOOKS ARE ALIKE IN MANY WAYS, THE FACTS HAVE BEEN COMBINED HERE TO TELL ONE STORY.

TO EVERYONE, JESUS SAYS-- I AM THE WAY... NO ONE CAN COME TO GOD BUT BY ME.

FOR ALMOST SIXTY YEARS PALESTINE, THE HOME OF THE JEWS, HAS BEEN RULED BY THE MIGHTY ROMAN EMPIRE. TO MAINTAIN THEIR CONTROL, THE ROMANS APPOINTED HEROD, A CLEVER BUT CRUEL MAN, TO RULE THE LAND. THE JEWS HATE HIM -- AND THE ROMAN OFFICIALS WHO COME TO HIS COURT. THE TIME IS NOW 6 B.C....

HERE, OLD MAN, CARRY THIS FOR ME.

THAT CHEST IS TOO HEAVY FOR SUCH AN OLD MAN.

THE ROMANS DON'T CARE.

HOURS LATER THE OLD MAN REACHES HOME...

GRANDFATHER! WHAT'S THE MATTER?

A ROMAN SOLDIER MADE HIM CARRY A HEAVY CHEST TO HEROD'S PALACE.

5

THAT AFTERNOON--AS THE JEWS IN JERUSALEM GATHER IN THE TEMPLE FOR PRAYER--AN OLD PRIEST, ZACHARIAS, ENTERS THE HOLY PLACE TO PRAY AND OFFER INCENSE.

THIS IS THE GREATEST DAY IN MY LIFE. AFTER ALL THESE YEARS IT IS FINALLY MY TURN TO OFFER INCENSE ON GOD'S HOLY ALTAR.

HE STAYS SO LONG IN THE SECRET ROOM THAT THE PEOPLE BEGIN TO WONDER.

ZACHARIAS' PRAYER IS LONGER THAN THAT OF MOST PRIESTS.

HE IS A GOOD MAN. IT'S TOO BAD HE HAS NO SON TO TAKE HIS PLACE.

AT LAST ZACHARIAS COMES OUT AND FACES THE PEOPLE--BUT HE CANNOT SPEAK!

WHAT HAPPENED IN THE HOLY PLACE OF GOD?

# A Secret from God

FROM LUKE 1: 23-55

ZACHARIAS, THE AGED PRIEST, HAS NOT SPOKEN A WORD SINCE HE ENTERED THE HOLY PLACE OF THE TEMPLE TO OFFER INCENSE. MOST OF THE PEOPLE IN JERUSALEM BELIEVE HE SAW A VISION, BUT ZACHARIAS MAKES NO EXPLANATION. HE COMPLETES HIS TIME OF SERVICE IN THE TEMPLE, AND RETURNS TO HIS HOME IN THE HILLS OF JUDAH. HIS WIFE, ELISABETH, MEETS HIM AT THE DOOR...

ZACHARIAS! WHAT IS WRONG? WHY DON'T YOU SPEAK TO ME?

QUICKLY ZACHARIAS WRITES HIS ANSWER AND HANDS IT TO ELISABETH TO READ.

WHILE I WAS PRAYING IN THE HOLY PLACE, AN ANGEL SPOKE TO ME. HE TOLD ME THAT WE WOULD HAVE A SON. HIS NAME WILL BE JOHN, AND HE WILL PREPARE OUR PEOPLE FOR THE DELIVERER FROM GOD.

A SON! AND HE WILL PREPARE THE WAY FOR GOD'S CHOSEN ONE!

BUT, ZACHARIAS, WHY DO YOU WRITE THIS INSTEAD OF TELLING ME?

ZACHARIAS WRITES A SECOND MESSAGE AND GIVES IT TO HIS WIFE.

GOD FORGIVE ME. I DOUBTED THE ANGEL'S MESSAGE, AND HE TOLD ME I WOULD NOT BE ABLE TO SPEAK UNTIL THE MESSAGE CAME TRUE.

Overjoyed--and awed by the great trust God has placed in them-- Zacharias and Elisabeth prepare for the birth of their son. In the months that pass they often read together the parts of scripture that tell about God's promises to his people.

DO NOT BE AFRAID, MARY. GOD HAS CHOSEN YOU TO BE THE MOTHER OF HIS SON. HIS NAME WILL BE "JESUS." HE WILL BE A KING WHOSE REIGN WILL NEVER END.

I AM THE LORD'S SERVANT AND I WILL DO WHATEVER HE SAYS.

As the aged priest and his wife wait for the coming of their son, the angel Gabriel appears to Elisabeth's cousin Mary, who is engaged to Joseph, a carpenter, in Nazareth.

8

MARY TELLS NO ONE OF THE ANGEL'S MESSAGE, BUT IN A FEW DAYS SHE GOES TO THE CARPENTER SHOP TO SEE JOSEPH.

I HAVE DECIDED TO GO AND VISIT MY COUSIN, ELISABETH.

IN JUDAH? I HATE TO HAVE YOU GO ALONE, MARY. IF ONLY THE PERIOD OF OUR ENGAGEMENT WERE OVER AND WE WERE MARRIED. THEN I COULD TAKE YOU THERE.

BUT, MARY LEAVES NAZARETH ALONE.

THE ANGEL SAID THAT ELISABETH IS GOING TO HAVE A SON, TOO. IT WILL BE GOOD TO TALK WITH HER.

AND WHEN SHE REACHES HER COUSIN...

MARY, HOW WONDERFULLY GOD HAS BLESSED YOU! BUT, TELL ME, WHY HAS THE MOTHER OF MY LORD COME TO VISIT ME?

FROM THIS GREETING MARY KNOWS THAT ELISABETH SHARES HER WONDERFUL SECRET. JOYFULLY SHE SINGS ALOUD HER PRAISE TO GOD.

MY SOUL DOTH MAGNIFY THE LORD... FOR HE THAT IS MIGHTY HATH DONE TO ME GREAT THINGS; AND HOLY IS HIS NAME.

# A Father's Prophecy

FROM LUKE 1:57-80; 2:1-5

THE DAYS PASS SWIFTLY IN THE HOME OF THE OLD PRIEST, ZACHARIAS. HIS WIFE, ELISABETH, AND HER YOUNG COUSIN, MARY, SPEND MANY HOURS TALKING ABOUT THE SONS GOD HAS PROMISED THEM. WHEN ELISABETH AND ZACHARIAS' CHILD IS BORN, NEIGHBORS AND RELATIVES COME TO SEE HIM.

HOW PROUD ZACHARIAS MUST BE TO HAVE A SON TO BEAR HIS NAME.

HE IS PROUD TO HAVE A SON, BUT, THE CHILD'S NAME IS JOHN.

JOHN? THEN YOU AREN'T NAMING HIM FOR ANYONE IN YOUR FAMILY?

ZACHARIAS -- WHO HAS NOT BEEN ABLE TO SPEAK A WORD SINCE HE DOUBTED THE ANGEL'S MESSAGE ABOUT THE BIRTH OF HIS SON -- MOTIONS FOR A TABLET. QUICKLY HE WRITES HIS ANSWER, AND HANDS IT TO THE WOMAN TO READ.

HIS NAME IS JOHN.

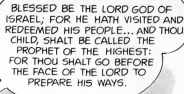

SO THE BABY IS NAMED ACCORDING TO THE INSTRUCTIONS OF THE ANGEL-- AND AT THAT MOMENT ZACHARIAS IS ABLE TO SPEAK.

BLESSED BE THE LORD GOD OF ISRAEL; FOR HE HATH VISITED AND REDEEMED HIS PEOPLE... AND THOU, CHILD, SHALT BE CALLED THE PROPHET OF THE HIGHEST: FOR THOU SHALT GO BEFORE THE FACE OF THE LORD TO PREPARE HIS WAYS.

ON THEIR WAY HOME THE PEOPLE TALK ABOUT THE STRANGE EVENTS CONNECTED WITH THE BIRTH OF ZACHARIAS' SON.

THE NAME JOHN --WHAT DOES IT MEAN?

IT MEANS, "GOD HAS BEEN GRACIOUS." GOD MUST HAVE A SPECIAL PURPOSE FOR THAT CHILD.

HOME AGAIN IN NAZARETH, MARY THINKS ABOUT THE PURPOSE GOD HAS FOR HER CHILD. BUT JOSEPH, THE CARPENTER TO WHOM SHE IS ENGAGED, DOES NOT UNDERSTAND WHAT THE ANGEL HAS TOLD MARY ABOUT THE SON THAT IS TO BE BORN. ONE NIGHT AN ANGEL COMES TO HIM.

GOD HAS CHOSEN MARY TO BE THE MOTHER OF HIS SON. YOU MUST CALL THE CHILD JESUS, FOR HE WILL SAVE HIS PEOPLE FROM THEIR SINS.

EARLY THE NEXT MORNING, JOSEPH HURRIES TO SEE MARY.

O MARY, IN A DREAM LAST NIGHT AN ANGEL TOLD ME THAT YOU ARE TO BE THE MOTHER OF THE LORD. I SEE NOW THAT GOD HAS CHOSEN ME TO TAKE CARE OF YOU AND YOUR SON.

SO MARY AND JOSEPH ARE MARRIED, AND MOVE INTO JOSEPH'S HOUSE BESIDE THE CARPENTER SHOP. IN THE EVENINGS WHEN THE DAY'S WORK IS DONE, THEY REST ON THE ROOF TOP--WATCHING THE STARS AND TALKING ABOUT GOD'S PROMISE TO MARY.

BUT ONE DAY JOSEPH COMES HOME FROM THE MARKET PLACE WITH BAD NEWS: CAESAR AUGUSTUS HAS ORDERED EVERYONE TO REGISTER HIS NAME AND PROPERTY. SINCE JOSEPH AND MARY ARE DESCENDANTS OF KING DAVID, JOSEPH MUST GO TO BETHLEHEM, THE CITY OF DAVID.

BUT I CAN'T GO NOW-- AND LEAVE YOU...

YOU MUST GO, JOSEPH, AND I'LL GO WITH YOU. DON'T WORRY--GOD WILL BE WITH US.

EAGER TO HAVE THE REGISTRATION OVER, THEY SET OUT. SOON OTHERS JOIN THEM ON THE WAY. BUT THE JOURNEY TAKES SEVERAL DAYS, AND AFTER A WHILE JOSEPH AND MARY FALL BEHIND-- UNTIL THEY ARE AMONG THE LAST TO REACH BETHLEHEM.

WE HAVE TRAVELED A LONG WAY AND MY WIFE IS VERY TIRED. I NEED A ROOM.

I'M SORRY, BUT BETHLEHEM IS CROWDED THESE DAYS. THERE'S NO ROOM HERE.

12

# The Night the Angels Sang

FROM LUKE 1: 23-55

AFTER A TIRESOME JOURNEY FROM NAZARETH, JOSEPH AND MARY REACH BETHLEHEM. BUT THE CITY IS SO CROWDED THAT THERE IS NO ROOM FOR THEM IN THE INN.

MY WIFE IS GOING TO HAVE A CHILD -- SOON. HAVE YOU NO PLACE SHE CAN GO TO REST?

NOT THIS NIGHT. BUT, WAIT -- THERE IS AN EMPTY PLACE IN MY STABLE, IF--

TAKE IT, JOSEPH. IT IS LATE, AND I'M VERY TIRED.

MARY, THIS IS NO PLACE FOR YOU.

IT'S ALL RIGHT, JOSEPH. I'M THANKFUL FOR WHATEVER SHELTER WE CAN FIND.

THAT SAME NIGHT SOME SHEPHERDS ARE WATCHING THEIR SHEEP ON THE HILLS OUTSIDE THE CITY. THEY TALK OF THE CROWDS THAT HAVE COME TO BETHLEHEM.

SUDDENLY-- A GREAT LIGHT SHINES AROUND THE SHEPHERDS.

I'VE HEARD THAT CAESAR AUGUSTUS ORDERED THIS REGISTRATION SO THAT HE CAN COLLECT MORE TAXES. WILL WE NEVER BE FREE FROM THESE FOREIGN TYRANTS?

GOD HAS PROMISED US A DELIVERER. AND ALL MY LIFE I HAVE PRAYED THAT I WOULD LIVE TO SEE HIM.

WHAT IS IT?

O GOD, PROTECT US.

FEAR NOT; FOR I BRING YOU GOOD NEWS OF GREAT JOY FOR ALL THE PEOPLE. FOR TO YOU IS BORN IN THE CITY OF DAVID A SAVIOR, WHO IS CHRIST THE LORD. YOU WILL FIND THE BABY LYING IN A MANGER.

THEN THE SKY IS FILLED WITH A GREAT CHOIR OF ANGELS -- SINGING THEIR PRAISE TO GOD.

*Glory to God in the highest, and on earth peace, good will toward men.*

THE ANGELS LEAVE -- THE BEAUTIFUL LIGHT DISAPPEARS. ONCE AGAIN IT IS DARK AND STILL ON THE BETHLEHEM HILLS.

I CAN SCARCELY BELIEVE WHAT I HAVE SEEN AND HEARD. GOD HAS SENT OUR DELIVERER, OUR SAVIOR -- **TONIGHT!**

AND TO THINK HE SENT HIS ANGEL TO TELL POOR SHEPHERDS LIKE US!

THE ANGEL SAID WE WOULD FIND THE SAVIOR IN A MANGER. LET'S GO TO BETHLEHEM AND SEE HIM.

EAGERLY -- AND WITH AWE AND WONDER -- THE SHEPHERDS HURRY TO BETHLEHEM. INSIDE THE GATE THEY TURN TOWARD THE INN...

LOOK -- THERE'S A LIGHT IN THE STABLE!

OUR SAVIOR IS HERE! AND I'M GOING TO SEE HIM!

# A King Is Born

FROM LUKE 2:7, 16-20; MATTHEW 2:1-8

IT IS A STRANGE AND HOLY NIGHT. WHILE THE CROWDED CITY OF BETHLEHEM SLEEPS, THE SON OF GOD IS BORN. LOVINGLY, MARY WRAPS HER BABY IN SWADDLING CLOTHES AND LAYS HIM IN A MANGER... AND THERE THE SHEPHERDS FIND HIM.

AN ANGEL TOLD US THAT THE SAVIOR HAS BEEN BORN. MAY WE SEE HIM?

MARY NODS, AND JOSEPH TURNS THE LAMP A LITTLE SO THAT ITS LIGHT FALLS ON THE MANGER. REVERENTLY THE SHEPHERDS LOOK AT THE BABY JESUS.

O GOD, WE THANK THEE FOR SENDING OUR SAVIOR, AND FOR LETTING US SEE HIM.

QUIETLY, THE SHEPHERDS TURN AWAY...

...AND GO BACK TO THEIR FLOCKS, STILL PRAISING GOD FOR WHAT HAS HAPPENED THAT NIGHT. AT THE SAME TIME IN A LAND FAR TO THE EAST, WISE MEN TALK ABOUT A STRANGE THING THEY HAVE JUST SEEN.

THAT NEW STAR-- IT'S BRIGHTER THAN ALL THE REST. IT MUST HAVE A SPECIAL MEANING.

IT IS A SIGN FROM GOD THAT THE GREAT KING OF THE JEWS HAS BEEN BORN.

LET US GO TO JERUSALEM AND FIND THE KING.

AFTER MONTHS OF TRAVEL, THE WISE MEN REACH JERUSALEM.

WE HAVE COME TO WORSHIP THE ONE BORN TO BE KING OF THE JEWS. PLEASE TELL US WHERE WE CAN FIND HIM.

YOU MUST BE MISTAKEN. NO KING HAS BEEN BORN HERE RECENTLY.

17

WHEN THE WISE MEN INQUIRE AT THE PALACE, KING HEROD-- WHO HAS COMMITTED MORE THAN ONE MURDER TO PROTECT HIS THRONE-- IS FRIGHTENED. HE CALLS FOR THE CHIEF PRIESTS AND SCRIBES.

IS THERE ANYTHING IN THE SACRED BOOKS TELLING ABOUT A BABY WHO WILL BECOME KING OF THE JEWS?

YES, THE SCRIPTURES SAY HE WILL BE BORN IN BETHLEHEM.

SECRETLY HEROD SENDS FOR THE WISE MEN AND ASKS THEM WHEN THEY SAW THE STAR AND HOW LONG IT TOOK THEM TO COME TO JERUSALEM. THEN HE SPEAKS VERY SLYLY.

LOOK FOR THE CHILD IN BETHLEHEM. WHEN YOU FIND HIM, COME BACK AND TELL ME WHERE HE IS SO THAT I MAY WORSHIP HIM, TOO.

AND WHEN I FIND THAT CHILD, I'LL KILL HIM. NO ONE IS GOING TO BE KING OF THE JEWS BUT ME!

# Flight in the Night

FROM MATTHEW 2:9-14

FOLLOWING HEROD'S INSTRUCTIONS, THE WISE MEN SET OUT FOR BETHLEHEM. AS THEY LEAVE JERUSALEM, THEY AGAIN SEE THE STAR THEY HAD SEEN IN THE EAST. IT LEADS THEM TO BETHLEHEM, AND THERE...

LOOK! THE STAR HAS STOPPED ABOVE THAT HOUSE!

OUR JOURNEY IS FINISHED! SOON WE'LL SEE THE CHILD WHO IS TO BE KING OF THE JEWS!

PEOPLE IN BETHLEHEM ARE SURPRISED TO SEE THE IMPORTANT-LOOKING STRANGERS STOP BEFORE THE HOUSE WHERE JOSEPH AND MARY NOW LIVE. WHEN THE WISE MEN TELL THEIR REASON FOR COMING, THEY ARE INVITED INSIDE. THERE THEY KNEEL BEFORE THE BABY JESUS.

WE HAVE COME A LONG WAY TO WORSHIP THE ROYAL CHILD.

AND TO BRING HIM GIFTS OF GOLD, FRANKINCENSE, AND MYRRH.

THAT NIGHT AT THE INN THE WISE
MEN MAKE PLANS FOR THEIR
RETURN HOME.

I'M GLAD THAT WE CAN
GO BACK TO JERUSALEM
AND TELL KING HEROD
WHERE HE CAN FIND
THE BABY.

THE NEXT MORNING...

I HAD A
DREAM—

SO DID I! IN MY DREAM
GOD WARNED US NOT TO
RETURN TO JERUSALEM
BECAUSE HEROD IS
JEALOUS AND WANTS
TO KILL THE CHILD.

I HAD THE SAME DREAM!
HEROD WILL FIND OUT
NOTHING FROM US.
WE'LL GO HOME BY
ANOTHER ROUTE.

20

BUT THE WISE MEN ARE NOT THE ONLY ONES WHO ARE WARNED OF HEROD'S ANGER. AN ANGEL OF GOD APPEARS TO JOSEPH, TOO...

MARY! AN ANGEL HAS TOLD ME WE MUST ESCAPE AT ONCE -- TO EGYPT. HEROD WANTS TO KILL JESUS.

KILL JESUS! OH, NO!

IN THE MIDDLE OF THE NIGHT, JOSEPH AND MARY WITH THE BABY JESUS STEAL QUIETLY OUT OF THE CITY.

IN JERUSALEM, HEROD WAITS FOR THE RETURN OF THE WISE MEN. WHEN THEY DO NOT COME, HE SUSPECTS THEY ARE TRYING TO PROTECT THE CHILD -- FROM HIM.

THAT CHILD WILL NEVER LIVE TO TAKE **MY** THRONE. I'LL KILL EVERY BABY IN BETHLEHEM BEFORE I LET HIM ESCAPE.

# Boy in the Temple

FROM MATTHEW 2:16-23; LUKE 2:40-52

FEARING THAT THE BABY JESUS WILL TAKE HIS THRONE, HEROD ORDERS ALL BOY BABIES IN BETHLEHEM KILLED. BUT JOSEPH AND MARY ESCAPE WITH JESUS TO EGYPT. AFTER A FEW MONTHS, AN ANGEL TELLS JOSEPH THAT HEROD IS DEAD AND THAT IT IS NOW SAFE TO TAKE JESUS HOME. IN NAZARETH...

MARY! AND JOSEPH! HOW GOOD TO HAVE YOU BACK. WHAT IS THE BABY'S NAME?

HIS NAME IS JESUS.

JESUS. THE NAME MEANS "GOD SAVES." WE NEED SOMEONE TO SAVE US FROM THE TYRANTS WHO RULE PALESTINE.

JOSEPH SETS UP HIS CARPENTER SHOP--AND AS THE YEARS PASS, JESUS LEARNS TO HELP HIM. WHEN THE DAY'S WORK IS OVER JESUS LISTENS TO THE ELDERS OF THE TOWN...

IN THE DAYS OF KING DAVID, **WE** WERE THE RULERS.

YES, BUT IN THOSE DAYS PEOPLE OBEYED GOD. TODAY, TOO MANY IGNORE HIS LAWS.

BUT JOSEPH AND MARY OBEY GOD'S COMMANDMENTS, AND TEACH JESUS TO OBEY THEM, TOO. EACH SPRING THEY ATTEND THE PASSOVER FEAST IN JERUSALEM TO THANK GOD FOR DELIVERING THEIR ANCESTORS FROM SLAVERY IN EGYPT. IN THE CARAVAN THAT MAKES THE ANNUAL JOURNEY FROM NAZARETH, THERE IS NO ONE MORE EXCITED THAN JESUS.

THIS YEAR, AS HE WORSHIPS IN THE TEMPLE, JESUS THINKS OF MANY QUESTIONS HE WOULD LIKE TO ASK THE TEACHERS OF THE JEWS.

AFTER THE FEAST IS OVER, THE PEOPLE SET OUT FOR THEIR HOMES. THAT NIGHT WHEN THEY MAKE CAMP...

JOSEPH, WHERE IS JESUS?

HE'S WITH HIS FRIENDS. I'LL FIND HIM.

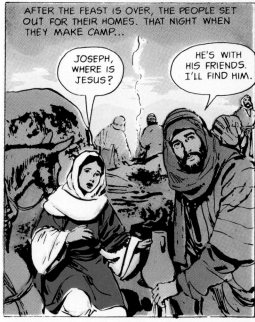

BUT NO ONE HAS SEEN JESUS. FRANTICALLY, JOSEPH AND MARY TURN BACK TO JERUSALEM. THEY SEARCH THE INNS, THE CROWDED STREETS, AND FINALLY THE TEMPLE.

JESUS! WE HAVE BEEN LOOKING FOR YOU EVERYWHERE.

BUT, MOTHER, DIDN'T YOU KNOW THAT I WOULD BE IN MY FATHER'S HOUSE?

WE ARE SURPRISED AT YOUR SON'S KNOWLEDGE OF THE SCRIPTURES. HIS QUESTIONS SHOW THAT HE HAS THOUGHT A GREAT DEAL ABOUT GOD AND HIS LAWS FOR MAN.

JESUS IS NOT LIKE ANYONE ELSE. EVEN I, HIS MOTHER, DO NOT UNDERSTAND EVERYTHING ABOUT HIM.

JESUS RETURNS WITH JOSEPH AND MARY TO NAZARETH, WHERE HE LIVES UNTIL HE IS 30 YEARS OLD. HE GROWS TALL AND STRONG, AND IS WELL LIKED BY THE PEOPLE OF NAZARETH. GOD IS ALSO PLEASED WITH HIM. SEVENTY MILES AWAY, IN THE WILDERNESS NEAR THE DEAD SEA, A MAN OF THE SAME AGE PREPARES FOR AN ASSIGNMENT THAT WAS PLANNED FOR HIM -- EVEN BEFORE HE WAS BORN.

# Tempted!

FROM LUKE 3: 1—4: 4

AS SOON AS JOHN, THE COUSIN OF JESUS, IS OLD ENOUGH TO UNDERSTAND, HIS FATHER TELLS HIM: "BEFORE YOU WERE BORN, GOD PLANNED FOR YOU TO SERVE HIM IN A SPECIAL WAY." JOHN GROWS UP PREPARING TO SERVE GOD. AND AFTER THE DEATH OF HIS PARENTS HE GOES INTO THE WILDERNESS TO PRAY AND STUDY. THERE GOD CALLS HIM TO BEGIN HIS WORK.

O GOD, I'M READY TO PREPARE THE WAY FOR THE COMING OF THE SAVIOR.

JOHN PUTS HIS WORDS INTO ACTION AND BEGINS PREACHING ALONG THE JORDAN RIVER.

REPENT OF YOUR SINS AND BE BAPTIZED, FOR GOD'S KINGDOM IS CLOSE AT HAND.

NEWS SPREADS FAR AND WIDE ABOUT THE MAN WHO LOOKS AND SPEAKS LIKE A PROPHET OF OLD. CROWDS COME OUT FROM JERUSALEM TO HEAR THE MAN CALLED JOHN THE BAPTIST. SOME ARE ONLY CURIOUS, BUT JOHN KNOWS THEIR THOUGHTS.

DO YOU THINK THAT JUST BECAUSE YOU ARE JEWS YOU WILL BE ALLOWED IN GOD'S KINGDOM? NO, YOU MUST REPENT--

THE SCOFFERS TURN AWAY, BUT MANY PEOPLE LISTEN EAGERLY. ONE DAY A CROWD GATHERS AT THE JORDAN RIVER.

ARE YOU THE SAVIOR GOD HAS PROMISED US?

NO. I BAPTIZE WITH WATER, BUT HE WILL BAPTIZE WITH THE HOLY SPIRIT OF GOD. PREPARE YOURSELVES; THE SAVIOR IS COMING!

UNKNOWN TO JOHN, THE VERY ONE HE IS TALKING ABOUT IS IN THE CROWD. JESUS HAS COME DOWN FROM NAZARETH TO HEAR HIM. HE ASKS TO BE BAPTIZED.

WHY DO YOU COME TO **ME** FOR BAPTISM? IT IS **I** WHO NEED TO BE BAPTIZED BY YOU.

IT IS GOOD, JOHN, FOR US TO SHOW THAT WE BELONG TO GOD'S KINGDOM.

26

SO JOHN BAPTIZES JESUS. AND WHEN JESUS COMES UP OUT OF THE WATER, THE SPIRIT OF GOD DESCENDS LIKE A DOVE UPON HIM. THEN A VOICE FROM HEAVEN SPEAKS:

THIS IS MY BELOVED SON IN WHOM I AM WELL PLEASED.

THE CROWDS DO NOT UNDERSTAND WHAT HAS HAPPENED-- THEY GO HOME, NOT REALIZING THAT THEY HAVE SEEN THEIR SAVIOR. JOHN CONTINUES PREACHING -- REPENT OF YOUR SINS, FOR THE KINGDOM OF GOD IS COMING SOON.

TO JESUS, THE WORDS OF HIS FATHER ARE A SIGN OF APPROVAL, AND THE GIFT OF THE HOLY SPIRIT IS AN ASSURANCE OF HELP FOR THE WORK GOD HAS SENT HIM TO DO. HE GOES INTO THE WILDERNESS -- ALONE --TO THINK ABOUT HIS PLAN FOR ESTABLISHING GOD'S KINGDOM.

AT THE END OF FORTY DAYS, JESUS IS HUNGRY. AS HE THINKS OF FOOD, HE HEARS THE VOICE OF THE DEVIL TEMPTING HIM TO USE HIS DIVINE POWER FOR HIS OWN BENEFIT. "IF YOU ARE REALLY THE SON OF GOD," THE DEVIL SAYS, "TURN THIS STONE INTO BREAD. AFTER ALL, GOD WOULD NOT WANT HIS BELOVED SON TO BE HUNGRY."

SCRIPTURE SAYS, "MAN SHALL NOT LIVE BY BREAD ALONE, BUT BY THE WORD OF GOD."

THE DEVIL DOESN'T GIVE UP EASILY. HE TRIES AGAIN-- AND THIS TIME WITH A MORE POWERFUL TEMPTATION ...

27

# Victory in the Wilderness

To PREVENT JESUS FROM CARRYING OUT GOD'S WORK, THE DEVIL TEMPTS HIM TO SEEK EARTHLY POWERS FOR HIMSELF. BUT JESUS REFUSES. THE DEVIL TRIES AGAIN -- THIS TIME HE TEMPTS JESUS TO MAKE HIMSELF POPULAR BY DOING SOMETHING SENSATIONAL.

"LET PEOPLE SEE YOUR DIVINE POWER BY THROWING YOURSELF FROM THE ROOF OF THE TEMPLE," THE DEVIL SAYS. "FOR, IF YOU ARE THE SON OF GOD, HIS ANGELS WILL TAKE CARE OF YOU."

THE SCRIPTURES SAY, "THOU SHALT NOT TEMPT GOD."

HAVING REJECTED EVERY TEMPTATION, JESUS LEAVES THE WILDERNESS AND GOES BACK TO BETHANY BEYOND THE JORDAN.

AS JESUS ENTERS BETHANY, JOHN THE BAPTIST POINTS HIM OUT TO TWO OF HIS OWN DISCIPLES --ANDREW AND JOHN.

THERE IS THE SAVIOR I HAVE BEEN TELLING YOU ABOUT.

THE TWO MEN TURN AND QUICKLY FOLLOW JESUS.

MASTER-- MAY WE TALK WITH YOU?

YES, COME WITH ME TO MY LODGING PLACE.

LISTENING TO JESUS IS SUCH A WONDERFUL EXPERIENCE THAT HOURS GO BY BEFORE ANDREW SUDDENLY REMEMBERS...

MY BROTHER! HE CAME DOWN HERE FROM CAPERNAUM WITH ME TO HEAR JOHN THE BAPTIST. I MUST FIND HIM AND BRING HIM TO SEE YOU.

ANDREW RUNS TO THE HOUSE WHERE HE AND HIS BROTHER ARE STAYING.

SIMON! I HAVE FOUND THE SAVIOR!

29

SIMON EAGERLY FOLLOWS ANDREW BACK THROUGH THE WINDING STREETS OF BETHANY.

THIS IS SIMON, MY BROTHER.

YES, YOU ARE SIMON, BUT FROM NOW ON YOU SHALL BE CALLED PETER, BECAUSE YOU WILL BE LIKE A ROCK.

THE NEXT DAY JESUS GOES NORTH TO GALILEE. HE INVITES ANOTHER YOUNG MAN, PHILIP, TO BE HIS DISCIPLE AND GO WITH HIM.

PHILIP ACCEPTS JESUS' INVITATION. LIKE ANDREW, HE WANTS TO SHARE HIS GOOD NEWS, SO HE HURRIES TO TELL A FRIEND.

NATHANAEL--COME WITH ME! I HAVE FOUND THE SAVIOR! HE IS JESUS OF NAZARETH.

NAZARETH? CAN ANYTHING GOOD COME FROM **THAT** TOWN?

IF WHAT YOU SAY IS TRUE, MEN WOULD GIVE UP EVERYTHING THEY HAVE TO FOLLOW HIM.

COME AND SEE FOR YOURSELF!

NATHANAEL SEES JESUS, BUT HE STILL DOESN'T BELIEVE. THEN JESUS SPEAKS...

# Six Jars of Water

FROM JOHN 1: 47-51; 2: 1-11, 23-25; 3: 1, 2

PHILIP IS SO EXCITED ABOUT SEEING JESUS THAT HE HURRIES TO TELL A FRIEND. "NATHANAEL, COME WITH ME. I HAVE FOUND THE SAVIOR!" NATHANAEL DOUBTS SUCH NEWS, BUT HE AGREES TO SEE FOR HIMSELF. AS THEY APPROACH JESUS...

BEHOLD, A MAN IN WHOM THERE IS NOTHING DECEITFUL.

HOW DO **YOU** KNOW ANYTHING ABOUT ME?

BEFORE PHILIP CALLED YOU, YOU WERE SITTING UNDER A FIG TREE THINKING ABOUT GOD. I SAW YOU THERE.

YOU **ARE** THE SAVIOR FOR WHOM WE HAVE WAITED SO LONG!

HAVING FOUND HIS SAVIOR, NATHANAEL FORGETS EVERYTHING ELSE AND JOINS JESUS AND HIS FRIENDS AS THEY TRAVEL NORTH TO GALILEE. AT THE CROSSROADS, PETER AND ANDREW TURN OFF TO THEIR HOME NEAR THE SEA OF GALILEE; THE OTHERS GO ON TO CANA.

WHEN THEY REACH THE TOWN THEY ARE GREETED BY A FRIEND OF JESUS.

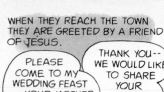

PLEASE COME TO MY WEDDING FEAST --YOUR MOTHER WILL BE THERE.

THANK YOU-- WE WOULD LIKE TO SHARE YOUR HAPPINESS.

DURING THE FEAST MARY DISCOVERS SOMETHING THAT WILL EMBARRASS THE GROOM--THERE IS NO MORE WINE. SHE TELLS JESUS, THEN SHE GOES TO THE SERVANTS.

DO WHATEVER HE TELLS YOU.

FILL THESE JARS WITH WATER.

WHY WATER? IT'S WINE WE NEED.

BUT THE SERVANTS SENSE A STRANGE AUTHORITY IN JESUS, AND THEY OBEY HIM.

NOW TAKE SOME TO THE HEADWAITER

WHY--IT IS WINE! IT'S A MIRACLE!

THIS MAN MUST BE A PROPHET OF GOD--NO ORDINARY MAN COULD DO SUCH A THING!

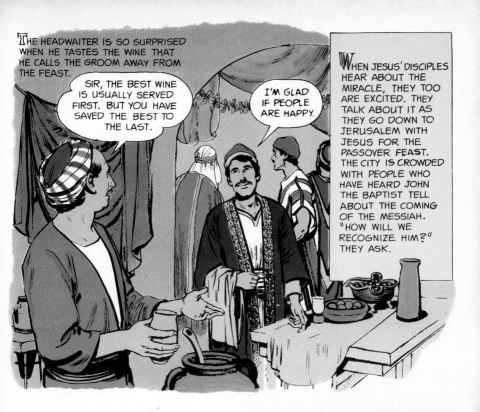

THE HEADWAITER IS SO SURPRISED WHEN HE TASTES THE WINE THAT HE CALLS THE GROOM AWAY FROM THE FEAST.

SIR, THE BEST WINE IS USUALLY SERVED FIRST. BUT YOU HAVE SAVED THE BEST TO THE LAST.

I'M GLAD IF PEOPLE ARE HAPPY.

WHEN JESUS' DISCIPLES HEAR ABOUT THE MIRACLE, THEY TOO ARE EXCITED. THEY TALK ABOUT IT AS THEY GO DOWN TO JERUSALEM WITH JESUS FOR THE PASSOVER FEAST. THE CITY IS CROWDED WITH PEOPLE WHO HAVE HEARD JOHN THE BAPTIST TELL ABOUT THE COMING OF THE MESSIAH. "HOW WILL WE RECOGNIZE HIM?" THEY ASK.

AS JESUS WALKS THROUGH THE BUSY STREETS, HE HEALS THE LAME AND THE SICK.

I CAN WALK! PRAISE BE TO GOD--THIS MAN HEALED ME!

BECAUSE OF THESE MIRACLES, PEOPLE BEGIN TO ASK: "IS JESUS THE MESSIAH?" ONE NIGHT, AFTER THE STREETS ARE EMPTY, A JUDGE OF THE JEWISH SUPREME COURT STEALS THROUGH THE STREETS OF JERU- SALEM ON A SECRET MISSION.

# The Judge's Problem

FROM JOHN 3:3—4:6

NICODEMUS, A JUDGE OF THE JEWISH SUPREME COURT, HAS A PROBLEM HE CAN'T SOLVE. PEOPLE IN JERUSALEM ARE ASKING, "IS JESUS THE SAVIOR WHO WILL OVERTHROW THE ROMANS AND SET UP GOD'S KINGDOM IN PALESTINE?"

NICODEMUS ISN'T SURE, AND HE WONDERS: "WHAT MUST A MAN DO TO ENTER GOD'S KINGDOM?" HE HAS TO FIND OUT. SO SECRETLY-- BY NIGHT-- HE GOES TO THE PLACE WHERE JESUS IS STAYING, AND JESUS ANSWERS HIS QUESTION EVEN BEFORE HE ASKS IT...

A MAN MUST BE BORN OVER AGAIN TO ENTER GOD'S KINGDOM.

BORN AGAIN? HOW CAN I BE BORN AGAIN WHEN I AM OLD?

YOU WERE BORN ONCE OF EARTHLY PARENTS. BUT YOU MUST BE BORN AGAIN OF GOD'S SPIRIT TO LIVE IN GOD'S KINGDOM.

I DON'T UNDERSTAND.

YOU CAN'T SEE THE WIND, CAN SEE WHAT IT DOES. YO SEE THE SPIRIT OF GOD, BUT TELL BY THE WAY A MAN LIV HE HAS BEEN BORN AGAIN A THE SPIRIT OF GOD IN HIS H GOD LOVES THE WORLD, AND HAS SENT ME TO GIVE THIS LIFE TO ALL WHO BELIEVE IN

SOMETIME LATE NEWS ABOU

NICODEMUS GOES AWAY -- STILL PUZZLED, BUT WANTING TO LEARN MORE ABOUT JESUS AND HIS TEACHINGS.

JESUS SEES THAT MANY OF THE PEOPLE IN JERUSALEM ARE NOT READY TO RECEIVE HIM AS THEIR SAVIOR, SO HE LEAVES THE CITY. IN JUDEA HE TELLS THE PEOPLE ABOUT GOD'S KINGDOM AND WHAT THEY MUST DO TO ENTER IT. HERE, THE PEOPLE LISTEN EAGERLY.

THIS TEACHER IS GREATER THAN ALL THE PROPHETS.

NEWS OF JESUS' SUCCESSFUL MINISTRY IN JUDEA REACHES JOHN THE BAPTIST.

I'VE HEARD THAT JESUS IS BECOMING MORE POPULAR EVERY DAY.

THANK GOD, I HAVE FULFILLED MY MISSION OF PREPARING THE WAY FOR HIM. JESUS' INFLUENCE MUST INCREASE, AND MINE DECREASE.

# In Enemy Territory

FROM JOHN 4:6-44; LUKE 4:16-28

THE JEWS AND SAMARITANS HAVE BEEN BITTER ENEMIES FOR OVER 500 YEARS, SO WHEN JESUS ASKS A SAMARITAN WOMAN FOR A DRINK OF WATER SHE IS SURPRISED.

WHAT? YOU, A JEW, ASK ME, A SAMARITAN, FOR A DRINK?

IF YOU KNEW WHO I AM YOU WOULD ASK ME TO GIVE YOU LIVING WATER.

BUT THE WELL IS DEEP AND YOU HAVE NO WAY TO GET WATER.

ANYONE WHO DRINKS FROM THIS WELL WILL THIRST AGAIN, BUT THE PERSON WHO DRINKS OF THE WATER I GIVE WILL NEVER THIRST, FOR IT IS GOD'S GIFT OF ETERNAL LIFE.

WHEN JESUS TELLS HER THAT HE IS THE SAVIOR FROM GOD, SHE BELIEVES HIM AND RUNS BACK TO THE TOWN TO TELL THE WONDERFUL NEWS.

COME! SEE A MAN WHO HAS TOLD ME THINGS ABOUT MY LIFE THAT NO STRANGER COULD KNOW. HE IS THE PROMISED MESSIAH! THE SAVIOR!

WHILE THE WOMAN IS IN THE TOWN, JESUS' DISCIPLES RETURN AND INVITE HIM TO SHARE THE FOOD THEY HAVE BOUGHT.

THANK YOU, BUT NOT NOW-- I HAVE FOOD THAT YOU DON'T KNOW ABOUT.

WHAT DO YOU MEAN?

MY FOOD IS TO DO THE WILL OF HIM WHO SENT ME. LOOK AT THE PEOPLE WHO ARE EAGER TO HEAR WHAT GOD HAS SENT ME TO TELL THEM.

ALTHOUGH THE SAMARITANS HATE JEWS, MANY OF THEM BELIEVE JESUS TO BE THEIR SAVIOR. "STAY," THEY PLEAD, "AND TELL US MORE ABOUT GOD AND HIS KINGDOM." JESUS REMAINS FOR TWO DAYS-- THEN GOES ON TO THE REGION OF GALILEE.

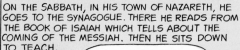

ON THE SABBATH, IN HIS TOWN OF NAZARETH, HE GOES TO THE SYNAGOGUE. THERE HE READS FROM THE BOOK OF ISAIAH WHICH TELLS ABOUT THE COMING OF THE MESSIAH. THEN HE SITS DOWN TO TEACH.

TODAY THIS SCRIPTURE HAS BEEN FULFILLED IN YOUR EARS.

YOU -- THE MESSIAH? WHY, YOU'RE JUST THE SON OF A NAZARETH CARPENTER!

NO PROPHET IS ACCEPTED IN HIS OWN COUNTRY. REMEMBER -- IN THE DAYS OF ELISHA THERE WERE MANY LEPERS IN ISRAEL, BUT THE PROPHET HEALED ONLY ONE -- A FOREIGNER, NAAMAN.

THE THOUGHT THAT GOD WOULD DO MORE FOR FOREIGNERS THAN FOR THEM -- HIS CHOSEN PEOPLE -- TURNS THE WORSHIPERS INTO AN ANGRY MOB.

DRIVE HIM OUT OF THE CITY!

KILL HIM!

BUT--SUDDENLY--JESUS TURNS AND LOOKS INTO THE FACES OF THE MEN AND WOMEN WHO HAVE KNOWN HIM FOR THIRTY YEARS. THEN HE WALKS--SLOWLY--THROUGH THEIR MIDST... AND, STRANGELY, NOT A PERSON DARES TO TOUCH HIM.

FROM NAZARETH JESUS GOES TO CAPERNAUM ON THE SEA OF GALILEE. THERE HE FINDS THE BROTHERS HE MET NEAR THE JORDAN RIVER.

PETER! ANDREW! COME WITH ME, AND I'LL MAKE YOU FISHERS OF MEN.

THEY LEAVE THEIR NETS AND GO AT ONCE WITH JESUS. FARTHER DOWN THE SHORE JESUS SEES TWO MORE FRIENDS--JAMES AND JOHN.

COME WITH ME AND BE MY DISCIPLES.

40

# Through the Roof

FROM MARK 2: 1-12

EVERYWHERE JESUS GOES THE CROWDS FOLLOW HIM. ONE DAY IN CAPERNAUM SO MANY PEOPLE CROWD INTO THE HOUSE WHERE HE IS TEACHING THAT NO ONE ELSE CAN ENTER. SOME MEN WHO HAVE BROUGHT A SICK FRIEND TO SEE JESUS CANNOT GET THROUGH THE CROWD, SO THEY CARRY THE MAN TO THE ROOF TOP.

MAKING A HOLE SO YOU CAN GET IN.

WHAT ARE YOU DOING?

AFTER A FEW MINUTES OF HARD WORK, THE SICK MAN IS LET DOWN THROUGH THE ROOF. JESUS IS PLEASED TO HELP, FOR HE KNOWS THE MAN'S REAL NEED.

YOUR SINS ARE FORGIVEN.

THE PEOPLE ARE AMAZED. BUT THE PHARISEES,* WHO HAVE COME OUT OF CURIOSITY TO HEAR JESUS, ARE ANGRY.

JESUS KNOWS WHAT THE PHARISEES ARE THINKING.

WHO IS THIS MAN WHO PRETENDS TO FORGIVE SINS?

HOW DARE HE ACT AS IF HE IS GOD!

WHICH IS EASIER-- TO SAY TO THE SICK, "YOUR SINS ARE FORGIVEN," OR TO SAY, "ARISE, TAKE UP YOUR BED, AND WALK"?

*The Pharisees are a group of Jews who believe in obeying not only the laws God gave to Moses but the hundreds of rules they have made--such as how far a man can walk on the Sabbath. Because Jesus is more concerned about helping people than obeying their rules, the Pharisees turn against him.

BUT SO THAT ALL MAY KNOW THAT I HAVE DIVINE POWER TO DO BOTH, I SAY TO YOU, "ARISE, TAKE UP YOUR BED, AND GO TO YOUR HOME."

MY SINS ARE FORGIVEN! I'M HEALED! GLORY BE TO GOD!

I'VE NEVER SEEN ANYTHING LIKE IT.

NEITHER HAVE I. BUT IF HE IS TRYING TO MAKE US THINK HE IS THE MESSIAH, WHY DOESN'T HE DO SOMETHING ABOUT OVERTHROWING THE ROMANS?

JESUS LEAVES THE HOUSE WHERE HE HAS BEEN TEACHING, AND AS HE PASSES BY THE TOLL HOUSE AT THE CITY GATE...

YOU TAX COLLECTORS ARE ALL ROBBERS. I CAN'T PAY THAT MUCH TAX, AND YOU KNOW IT.

YOU'D BETTER PAY IT! REMEMBER — I HAVE THE POWER OF THE WHOLE ROMAN EMPIRE BEHIND ME.

# One Man's Answer

FROM MATTHEW 9: 9-13; 12: 9-14

IN ALL CAPERNAUM THERE IS NO JEW MORE DESPISED THAN MATTHEW, A TAX COLLECTOR FOR ROME. ONE DAY AS HE AND A MERCHANT ARE ARGUING ABOUT TAXES ON A CARAVAN OF GOODS, JESUS PASSES BY. HE LOOKS STRAIGHT INTO THE EYES OF THE HATED TAX COLLECTOR...

MATTHEW, FOLLOW ME.

TO THE AMAZEMENT OF THE CROWD, MATTHEW TURNS FROM HIS WORK AND FOLLOWS JESUS.

I CAN'T BELIEVE IT! MATTHEW IS GIVING UP HIS JOB TO GO WITH A MAN OF GOD!

STRANGE -- NO GOOD JEW EVER WANTED MATTHEW FOR A FRIEND.

MATTHEW IS SO HAPPY TO START A NEW LIFE WITH JESUS THAT HE GIVES A BIG FEAST AND INVITES HIS FRIENDS TO MEET JESUS. SOME PHARISEES WHO ARE PASSING BY LOOK ON -- SURPRISED.

WHY DOES YOUR MASTER EAT WITH ALL THOSE SINNERS?

JESUS ANSWERS FOR HIS DISCIPLE.

ONLY THE SICK NEED A DOCTOR. I HAVE COME NOT TO CALL THE RIGHTEOUS BUT SINNERS TO REPENT.

THE PHARISEES HAVE NO ANSWER TO THIS -- BUT IT MAKES THEM EVEN MORE ANGRY. SO EVERYWHERE JESUS GOES THEY WATCH FOR A CHANCE TO CRITICIZE HIM. ONE SABBATH DAY IN THE SYNAGOGUE...

LOOK -- JESUS IS TALKING TO THAT MAN WITH THE WITHERED HAND. LET'S SEE IF WE CAN CATCH HIM BREAKING A SABBATH LAW. THEN WE'LL HAVE A CASE AGAINST HIM.

# Sermon on the Mount

FROM LUKE 6: 12-16; MATTHEW 5; 6; 7; 8: 5-13; 13: 45, 46;
MARK 4: 35-37

JESUS KNOWS THAT THE PHARISEES ARE PLOTTING TO TAKE HIS LIFE, BUT HE DOES NOT LET THIS KEEP HIM FROM CARRYING ON THE WORK GOD SENT HIM TO DO. HE GOES TO A NEARBY MOUNTAIN-- AND SPENDS THE NIGHT IN PRAYER...

...AND FATHER, I THANK THEE FOR GUIDING ME IN THE CHOICES I HAVE MADE THIS NIGHT.

IN THE MORNING HE CALLS HIS DISCIPLES TO HIM--AND FROM THE GROUP HE NAMES TWELVE TO BE HIS FULL-TIME HELPERS: SIMON PETER, ANDREW, JAMES, JOHN, PHILIP, NATHANAEL BARTHOLOMEW, MATTHEW, THOMAS, JAMES THE SON OF ALPHEUS, THADDEUS, SIMON THE ZEALOT, AND JUDAS ISCARIOT. THESE ARE KNOWN AS THE TWELVE APOSTLES.

As they come down the mountain they find a large crowd waiting for Jesus. So there--on the mountainside--Jesus preaches a sermon in which he explains what members of God's kingdom are like:

Blessed are the merciful: for they shall obtain mercy.
Blessed are the pure in heart: for they shall see God.
Blessed are the peacemakers: for they shall be called the children of God....
Ye are the light of the world.... Let your light so shine before men, that they may see your good works, and glorify your Father which is in heaven....
Love your enemies, bless them that curse you, do good to them that hate you, and pray for them which despitefully use you, and persecute you;
That ye may be the children of your Father which is in heaven: for he maketh his sun to rise on the evil and on the good, and sendeth rain on the just and on the unjust....
Therefore all things whatsoever ye would that men should do to you, do ye even so to them: for this is the law and the prophets.

(THE FULL SERMON IS FOUND IN MATTHEW, CHAPTERS 5, 6, 7.)

AFTER THE SERMON JESUS TAKES HIS DISCIPLES BACK TO CAPERNAUM. AS THEY ENTER THE CITY THEY ARE STOPPED BY AN OFFICER OF THE ROMAN ARMY.

JESUS! MY SERVANT IS ILL, WILL YOU PLEASE MAKE HIM WELL?

I WILL GO WITH YOU.

I'M NOT WORTHY TO HAVE YOU COME TO MY HOUSE -- BUT I KNOW THAT IF YOU SAY THE WORD MY SERVANT WILL BE HEALED.

NOWHERE IN ALL ISRAEL HAVE I SEEN A MAN WITH SUCH FAITH. GO BACK TO YOUR SERVANT -- AND AS YOU BELIEVE, SO IT WILL BE.

THE OFFICER HURRIES HOME.

MASTER! LOOK! I'M WELL. IT HAPPENED -- SUDDENLY -- JUST A FEW MINUTES AGO.

AREN'T YOU SURPRISED?

NO – BECAUSE I BELIEVED THAT JESUS WOULD HEAL YOU.

49

EVEN THOUGH THE PHARISEES ARE STILL PLOTTING AGAINST HIM, JESUS KEEPS ON TEACHING IN CAPERNAUM. ONE DAY THE CROWDS THAT COME TO HEAR HIM ARE SO GREAT THAT HE HAS TO GET INTO A BOAT AND PUSH OUT FROM SHORE IN ORDER TO TEACH THEM.

A MERCHANT ONCE SAW A RARE AND BEAUTIFUL PEARL. HE WANTED IT MORE THAN ANYTHING ELSE. SO HE SOLD EVERYTHING HE OWNED AND BOUGHT IT. THE KINGDOM OF GOD IS LIKE THAT PEARL--IT IS WORTH EVERYTHING YOU HAVE TO POSSESS IT.

WHEN EVENING COMES JESUS SUGGESTS TO HIS DISCIPLES THAT THEY CROSS OVER TO THE OTHER SIDE OF THE LAKE.

IT'S THE KIND OF A NIGHT WHEN A SUDDEN STORM COULD HIT.

# Mad Man by the Sea

FROM MARK 4: 37-41; 5: 1-24, 35-43

IN TERROR THE DISCIPLES RUSH TO THE STERN OF THE BOAT.

MASTER! DON'T YOU CARE IF WE DROWN?

JESUS RISES AND FACES THE STORMY SEA.

PEACE, BE STILL!

INSTANTLY THE WIND DIES AND THE WAVES VANISH.

WHO IS HE, THAT EVEN THE WINDS AND THE SEA OBEY HIM?

IN THE MORNING THE BOAT REACHES SHORE; AND AS JESUS AND HIS DISCIPLES ARE WALKING UP THE BEACH, A MAN POSSESSED BY AN EVIL SPIRIT RUSHES DOWN THE BANK TO MEET JESUS.

BE CAREFUL-- HE'S BROKEN HIS CHAINS.

COME OUT OF THE MAN, THOU UNCLEAN SPIRIT.

THE MAN IS CURED -- THE PEOPLE WHO SEE IT ARE AMAZED, AND THEY WONDER, TOO, WHAT POWER JESUS HAS TO MAKE EVIL SPIRITS OBEY HIM.

LET ME GO WITH YOU.

IT WOULD BE BETTER IF YOU WENT HOME AND TOLD YOUR FRIENDS WHAT GOD HAS DONE FOR YOU.

AFTER A WHILE JESUS AND HIS DISCIPLES RETURN TO CAPERNAUM. ONCE AGAIN A CROWD GATHERS TO HEAR HIM. BUT JUST AS JESUS BEGINS TO TEACH, JAIRUS, THE CHIEF RULER OF THE SYNAGOGUE, PUSHES HIS WAY THROUGH THE CROWD AND FALLS AT JESUS' FEET.

MY LITTLE GIRL — SHE'S DYING! PLEASE COME!

JESUS GOES WITH JAIRUS -- BUT ON THE WAY THEY ARE MET BY A SERVANT FROM JAIRUS' HOUSEHOLD...

IT'S TOO LATE -- YOUR DAUGHTER IS DEAD!

# The Mocking Crowd

FROM MARK 5:38-43; MATTHEW 9:35—11:1;
14:1-12; JOHN 6:1-10

WHEN JESUS AND HIS DISCIPLES REACH THE HOME OF JAIRUS, THEY FIND A CROWD OF PEOPLE WEEPING BECAUSE JAIRUS' DAUGHTER IS DEAD.

WHY ARE YOU CRYING? THE LITTLE GIRL IS JUST ASLEEP.

ASLEEP? HOW DARE YOU RAISE FALSE HOPE FOR THIS FAMILY? THE CHILD IS DEAD, AND EVERYONE KNOWS IT!

QUIETLY JESUS LEADS THE CHILD'S PARENTS INTO HER ROOM. THERE HE TAKES THE GIRL'S HAND AND SAYS, "ARISE." INSTANTLY SHE GETS UP-- AND LOOKS AT JESUS IN SURPRISE AND WONDER.

GIVE HER SOMETHING TO EAT-- BUT DO NOT TELL ANYONE WHAT HAS HAPPENED IN THIS ROOM.

BUT JAIRUS IS AN IMPORTANT MAN. NEWS ABOUT HIS DAUGHTER SPREADS QUICKLY. AND AS JESUS TRAVELS THROUGH GALILEE, PREACHING AND HEALING, HIS FAME INCREASES. THE PHARISEES WATCH ANGRILY. AS YET THEY HAVE NO REAL CASE AGAINST JESUS AND WITH-OUT ONE THEY DARE NOT STIR UP THE EXCITED CROWDS THAT FOLLOW HIM.

BUT JESUS IS CONCERNED ABOUT THE MANY PEOPLE WHO STILL HAVE NOT HEARD HIS MESSAGE. HE CALLS HIS DISCIPLES ASIDE.

THE PEOPLE ARE LIKE SHEEP WITHOUT A SHEPHERD. I WANT YOU TO GO OUT BY TWOS TO PREACH AND HEAL THE SICK AS I HAVE DONE. DO NOT BE WORRIED ABOUT WHAT TO SAY, FOR THE SPIRIT OF GOD WILL SPEAK THROUGH YOU.

THE DISCIPLES PREACH THROUGHOUT GALILEE. WHEN THEY RETURN JESUS PREPARES TO TAKE THEM TO A QUIET PLACE TO REST AND TALK ABOUT FUTURE PLANS. AS THEY ARE STARTING, A DISCIPLE OF JOHN THE BAPTIST BRINGS THEM TRAGIC NEWS.

JOHN HAS BEEN BEHEADED BY KING HEROD!

HEROD IS A WICKED MAN. BUT THIS IS THE WORST OF HIS SINS.

NO GREATER PROPHET THAN JOHN EVER LIVED. HE SPENT HIS LIFE DOING THE WILL OF GOD.

SORROWFULLY, JESUS AND HIS DISCIPLES CROSS THE LAKE AND GO UP ON A MOUNTAINSIDE, HOPING TO BE ALONE. BUT A GREAT CROWD FOLLOWS THEM AND JESUS STOPS TO TEACH AND HEAL THE SICK. LATE IN THE AFTERNOON...

PHILIP -- WHERE CAN WE BUY FOOD FOR THESE PEOPLE?

FOR **ALL** OF THEM? WHY, THERE MUST BE 5,000 MEN -- BESIDES THE WOMEN AND CHILDREN.

HERE'S A BOY WITH FIVE LOAVES OF BREAD AND TWO FISHES -- BUT WHAT GOOD IS THAT FOR SUCH A CROWD?

HAVE THE PEOPLE SIT DOWN AND GIVE THE FOOD TO ME.

# No Earthly Throne

FROM JOHN 6:10-15; MATTHEW 14:23-30

IT IS LATE AFTERNOON. THE CROWD THAT HAS FOLLOWED JESUS IS HUNGRY. BUT THE ONLY FOOD AVAILABLE BELONGS TO A BOY. HE EAGERLY GIVES IT TO JESUS, WHO THANKS GOD FOR IT AND HANDS IT TO HIS DISCIPLES.

DISTRIBUTE THE FOOD TO EVERYONE.

HOW FAR WILL FIVE LOAVES AND TWO FISHES GO IN FEEDING A CROWD OF OVER FIVE THOUSAND?

BUT THE DISCIPLES HAVE FAITH IN JESUS... AND THEY OBEY HIM.

LOOK! EVERYONE HERE IS GETTING ALL THE FOOD HE WANTS.

IT'S A MIRACLE!

WHEN THE PEOPLE HAVE FINISHED EATING, JESUS TURNS AGAIN TO HIS DISCIPLES.

GATHER UP THE FOOD THAT REMAINS.

TWELVE BASKETS OF FOOD ARE LEFT OVER! THE PEOPLE ARE NOW MORE AMAZED THAN EVER.

MAYBE JESUS IS THE KING THE PROPHETS TALKED ABOUT.

A KING LIKE DAVID -- WHO WILL DESTROY OUR ENEMIES AND MAKE US RICH AND POWERFUL!

UT GOD SENT JESUS TO BE THE SAVIOR, TO BRING MEN INTO THE KINGDOM OF GOD -- NOT TO COMMAND ARMIES AND CONQUER THRONES. WHEN JESUS SEES THAT THE CROWD WANTS TO FORCE HIM TO BE A KING, HE QUICKLY CALLS HIS DISCIPLES.

LAUNCH THE BOAT AND CROSS OVER TO THE OTHER SIDE OF THE SEA. I WILL JOIN YOU LATER.

QUICKLY -- BEFORE THE EXCITEMENT OF THE PEOPLE GROWS STRONGER -- JESUS DISMISSES THEM. THEN HE GOES UP ON A MOUNTAIN TO PRAY. LATER THAT NIGHT -- ON THE SEA OF GALILEE...

THE WIND IS RISING! WE'RE IN FOR A STORM!

SOON THE STORM HITS...

HOW MUCH FARTHER TO LAND?

WE'RE ONLY HALF WAY.

SUDDENLY THEY LOOK UP TO SEE A FIGURE WALKING ON THE WATER. "A SPIRIT!" THEY CRY IN TERROR. ACROSS THE WAVES A CALM VOICE CALLS OUT: "IT IS I; DON'T BE AFRAID."

LORD! IF IT IS YOU, TELL ME TO COME TO YOU.

COME!

INSTANTLY PETER JUMPS FROM THE BOAT AND STARTS WALKING TOWARD JESUS. BUT WHEN HE SEES THE POWER OF THE WIND, HE LOSES FAITH-- AND BEGINS TO SINK...

# Miracle on the Sea

FROM MATTHEW 14: 30-36; JOHN 6: 22-71;
MARK 7: 1-23; MATTHEW 16: 13-26; 17: 1, 2

A STRONG NIGHT WIND IS STIRRING UP ANGRY WAVES ON THE SEA OF GALILEE. JESUS' DISCIPLES ARE ROWING HARD AGAINST THE STORM -- WHEN SUDDENLY THEY SEE A FIGURE WALKING TOWARD THEM. THEY ARE TERRIFIED -- UNTIL THEY SEE THAT THE MAN ON THE WATER IS JESUS. PETER GETS OUT OF THE BOAT AND STARTS TOWARDS JESUS -- BUT WHEN HE SEES THE ROUGH WAVES HE LOSES FAITH...

JESUS RESCUES PETER, AND AS THEY REACH THE BOAT, THE WIND DIES, AND THE SEA IS CALM.

ONLY SOMEONE FROM GOD COULD DO WHAT JESUS HAS DONE!

AT DAYBREAK THE DISCIPLES BRING THE BOAT TO SHORE. WHEN THE PEOPLE SEE JESUS, THEY HURRY TO BRING THEIR SICK AND CRIPPLED TO HIM. PATIENTLY AND LOVINGLY HE HEALS THEM ALL.

IF ONLY I CAN TOUCH HIS GARMENT I KNOW I WILL BE HEALED.

LATER THAT DAY JESUS GOES TO THE SYNAGOGUE IN CAPERNAUM. THE CROWD THAT HE FED THE DAY BEFORE IS THERE ASKING TO BE FED AGAIN. WHEN JESUS PREACHES A SERMON ABOUT THEIR SPIRITUAL NEEDS, MANY OF THEM ARE DISAPPOINTED AND TURN AWAY.

SEEING THIS, THE PHARISEES RESUME THEIR PUBLIC CRITICISM OF JESUS.

WE HAVE SEEN YOUR DISCIPLES EAT WITHOUT WASHING THEIR HANDS. WHY DO YOU LET THEM BREAK OUR LAWS AND DEFILE THEMSELVES?

NOTHING A MAN PUTS **INTO** HIS MOUTH CAN DEFILE HIM, BUT THE EVIL WORDS THAT COME **OUT** OF HIS MOUTH DEFILE HIM.

SHOCKED BECAUSE HE DEFENDS HIS DISCIPLES, THE PHARISEES TURN AWAY, MORE DETERMINED THAN EVER TO DESTROY JESUS.

DON'T YOU KNOW THAT YOU HAVE MADE THE PHARISEES ANGRY?

THE PHARISEES ARE BLIND TO THE WILL OF GOD—AND THEY ARE LEADING THE PEOPLE TO BE AS BLIND AS THEY ARE.

BECAUSE MOST OF THE PEOPLE WILL ACCEPT HIM ONLY AS AN EARTHLY KING, JESUS LEAVES GALILEE. HE TAKES HIS DISCIPLES TO THE COUNTRY OF PHENICIA— AND LATER TO THE REGION OF CAESAREA PHILIPPI, WHERE HE TEACHES THEM IN PRIVACY. THERE, ONE DAY, HE ASKS THEM: "WHO DO MEN SAY THAT I AM?"

JOHN THE BAPTIST... ELIJAH...

BUT WHO DO YOU SAY THAT I AM?

YOU ARE THE CHRIST, THE SON OF THE LIVING GOD.

BLESSED ARE YOU, PETER—FOR MY FATHER IN HEAVEN HAS REVEALED THIS TO YOU.

Now THAT THE DISCIPLES TRULY UNDERSTAND THAT HE IS THE PROMISED MESSIAH, JESUS TELLS THEM WHAT WILL HAPPEN WHEN HE GOES TO JERUSALEM.

THE PHARISEES AND PRIESTS DO NOT BELIEVE THAT I AM THE MESSIAH. THEY WILL HAVE ME KILLED—BUT IN THREE DAYS I WILL RISE AGAIN.

KILLED? NEVER!

PETER, YOU DO NOT UNDERSTAND GOD'S PLAN FOR ME. LET ME WARN ALL OF YOU-- IF YOU WANT TO FOLLOW ME, YOU MUST BE PREPARED TO SUFFER AS I WILL SUFFER.

IN SPITE OF WHAT JESUS TELLS THEM, THE DISCIPLES CANNOT BELIEVE THAT HE WILL BE PUT TO DEATH. THEY BELIEVE THAT HE HAS HELPED OTHERS, AND THAT HE WILL HELP HIMSELF. SEVERAL DAYS LATER, JESUS SPEAKS TO PETER, JAMES AND JOHN.

COME WITH ME UP THE MOUNTAIN.

I WONDER WHY...

AFTER A LONG CLIMB TO THE MOUNTAINTOP, JESUS GOES ASIDE TO PRAY. THE DISCIPLES SIT DOWN TO REST, BUT SOON FALL ASLEEP. WHEN THEY AWAKEN THEY SEE SOMETHING STRANGE AND GLORIOUSLY BEAUTIFUL...

# A Boy—and His Father's Faith

FROM MATTHEW 17: 3-13; MARK 9: 33; LUKE 9: 37-45

ALONE WITH JESUS ON THE MOUNTAIN, PETER, JAMES AND JOHN SEE HIM TRANSFIGURED. HIS FACE SHINES WITH THE BRIGHTNESS OF THE SUN -- HIS CLOTHES BECOME DAZZLING WHITE. THEN TWO GREAT MEN OF THE PAST, MOSES AND ELIJAH, APPEAR TO TALK WITH HIM.

BUT AS PETER SPEAKS A BRIGHT CLOUD DESCENDS ON THE MOUNTAINTOP... AND OUT OF THE CLOUD COMES THE VOICE OF GOD:

THIS IS MY BELOVED SON, IN WHOM I AM WELL PLEASED; HEAR YE HIM.

THE DISCIPLES ARE SO FRIGHTENED THAT THEY FALL TO THE GROUND BUT JESUS BENDS DOWN AND TOUCHES THEM...

DO NOT BE AFRAID.

THE NEXT MORNING--ON THE WAY DOWN THE MOUNTAIN--JESUS WARNS HIS DISCIPLES TO TELL NO ONE OF HIS TRANS-FIGURATION UNTIL AFTER HIS RESURRECTION. AFTER WHAT THEY HAVE JUST SEEN THE DISCIPLES CANNOT BELIEVE THAT JESUS WILL DIE -- SO THEY ARE PUZZLED WHEN JESUS TALKS ABOUT RISING FROM THE DEAD.

THEY REACH THE VAL-LEY TO FIND A GREAT CROWD GATHERED AROUND THE OTHER DISCIPLES.

AT THE SIGHT OF JESUS THE PEOPLE QUICKLY SURROUND HIM.

MY SON HAS SPELLS AND OFTEN FALLS INTO THE FIRE. I BROUGHT HIM TO YOUR DISCIPLES, BUT THEY COULD NOT HEAL HIM.

BRING YOUR SON TO ME.

THE FATHER OBEYS--BUT THE BOY HAS A SPELL AND FALLS TO THE GROUND AT JESUS' FEET.

IF YOU CAN HELP US-- PLEASE DO.

ALL THINGS ARE POSSIBLE TO ONE WHO HAS FAITH.

I BELIEVE! HELP ME, PLEASE, TO HAVE MORE FAITH.

THOU UNCLEAN SPIRIT--COME OUT OF THE BOY!

FOR A MOMENT THERE IS A STRUGGLE -- THEN THE BOY BECOMES SO STILL PEOPLE THINK HE IS DEAD. BUT JESUS REACHES DOWN TO TAKE HIS HAND.

ARISE!

INSTANTLY THE BOY GETS UP.

FATHER, WHAT HAPPENED?

YOU HAVE BEEN HEALED -- BY THE POWER OF GOD!

WHEN THEY ARE ALONE, THE DISCIPLES TURN TO JESUS.

WHY COULDN'T **WE** HEAL THE BOY?

YOU DID NOT HAVE FAITH. IF YOU HAVE FAITH THE SIZE OF A MUSTARD SEED, NOTHING IS IMPOSSIBLE FOR YOU.

LATER ON THE WAY TO CAPERNAUM, THE DISCIPLES TALK AMONG THEMSELVES ABOUT THE KINGDOM THEY EXPECT JESUS WILL SOON ESTABLISH. ALMOST AT ONCE THEY BEGIN TO QUARREL ABOUT WHICH ONE WILL BE THE GREATEST IN THAT KINGDOM.

IF ONLY **I** COULD SIT IN THE SEAT OF HONOR NEXT TO JESUS.

# Seventy Times Seven

**FROM MATTHEW 18:1-14, 21, 22;
JOHN 7:11-52; 8:21-59**

ON THE WAY TO CAPERNAUM THE DISCIPLES QUARREL ABOUT WHICH ONE OF THEM WILL BE THE MOST IMPORTANT PERSON IN THE KINGDOM THEY EXPECT JESUS TO ESTABLISH. WHEN THEY REACH THE CITY JESUS ASKS WHY THEY ARE QUARRELING AND THEY ARE ASHAMED TO SAY. HE CALLS A LITTLE CHILD TO HIM.

WHICHEVER ONE OF YOU WANTS TO BE GREATEST IN GOD'S KINGDOM MUST BE AS HUMBLE AND WILLING TO LEARN AS THIS LITTLE CHILD.

68

WHEN THE CHIEF PRIESTS AND PHARISEES HEAR WHAT THE PEOPLE ARE SAYING, THEY QUICKLY JOIN FORCES AGAINST JESUS.

IF WE DON'T GET RID OF HIM THE PEOPLE WILL ACCEPT HIM AS THE MESSIAH.

I'LL STOP HIM. CALL THE TEMPLE GUARDS

ARREST JESUS. BUT DO IT AT A TIME WHEN IT WILL CAUSE THE LEAST TROUBLE.

ON THE LAST DAY OF THE FEAST THE OFFICERS RETURN TO THE PRIESTS AND PHARISEES.

WHERE IS JESUS?

WE'VE NEVER HEARD ANYONE SPEAK AS THIS MAN DOES. WE COULD NOT ARREST HIM.

THE PRIESTS AND PHARISEES ARE FURIOUS -- BUT THEY ARE AFRAID TO FORCE THE ISSUE WHILE THE CITY IS FILLED WITH PEOPLE ATTENDING THE FEAST. BUT THE NEXT DAY...

JESUS RETURNS TO THE TEMPLE TO PREACH. IN THE COURSE OF HIS SERMON HE NOT ONLY POINTS OUT THE SINS OF THE PRIESTS AND PHARISEES BUT DECLARES THAT HE WAS WITH GOD EVEN BEFORE THE DAYS OF THEIR GREAT FOREFATHER, ABRAHAM.

HOW DARE HE CLAIM SUCH RELATIONSHIP WITH GOD!

STONE HIM! STONE HIM!

# A Jerusalem Beggar Meets the Son of God

FROM JOHN 9:1—10:21; LUKE 10:25

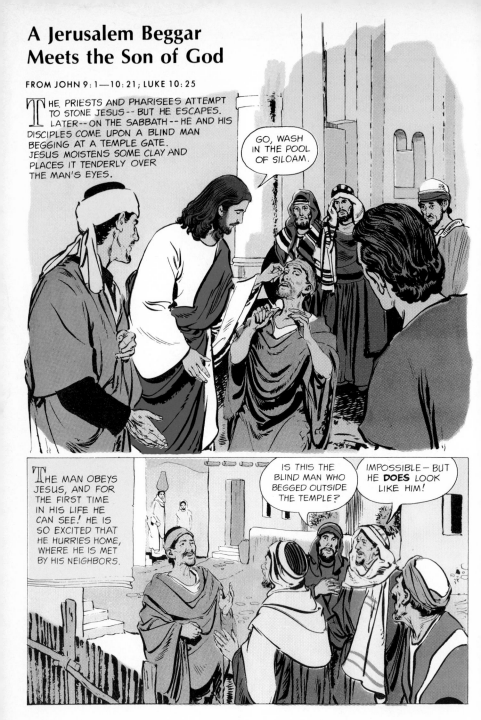

THE PRIESTS AND PHARISEES ATTEMPT TO STONE JESUS -- BUT HE ESCAPES. LATER -- ON THE SABBATH -- HE AND HIS DISCIPLES COME UPON A BLIND MAN BEGGING AT A TEMPLE GATE. JESUS MOISTENS SOME CLAY AND PLACES IT TENDERLY OVER THE MAN'S EYES.

GO, WASH IN THE POOL OF SILOAM.

THE MAN OBEYS JESUS, AND FOR THE FIRST TIME IN HIS LIFE HE CAN SEE! HE IS SO EXCITED THAT HE HURRIES HOME, WHERE HE IS MET BY HIS NEIGHBORS.

IS THIS THE BLIND MAN WHO BEGGED OUTSIDE THE TEMPLE?

IMPOSSIBLE — BUT HE **DOES** LOOK LIKE HIM!

BUT **I AM** THE MAN WHO WAS BLIND. JESUS GAVE ME MY SIGHT!

THE NEIGHBORS ARE WORRIED BECAUSE THE MAN HAS BEEN HEALED ON THE SABBATH. THEY TAKE HIM AT ONCE TO THE PHARISEES, WHO INTERPRET THE RULES ABOUT WHAT CAN BE DONE ON THE SABBATH.

THIS JESUS YOU TALK ABOUT IS A SINNER -- HE DOESN'T OBEY THE LAWS OF THE SABBATH.

I DO NOT KNOW WHETHER HE IS A SINNER, BUT THIS I DO KNOW: I WAS BLIND AND NOW I SEE.

THE PHARISEES TRY TO MAKE THE MAN TURN AGAINST JESUS, BUT THEY CANNOT, SO THEY PUT HIM OUT OF THE SYNAGOGUE. JESUS LEARNS WHAT HAS HAPPENED, AND SEARCHES FOR THE THE MAN. WHEN HE FINDS HIM THE PHARISEES QUICKLY GATHER AROUND.

DO YOU BELIEVE IN THE SON OF GOD?

WHO IS HE -- THAT I MAY BELIEVE IN HIM?

I AM -- THE VERY ONE WHO IS SPEAKING TO YOU.

LORD, I BELIEVE!

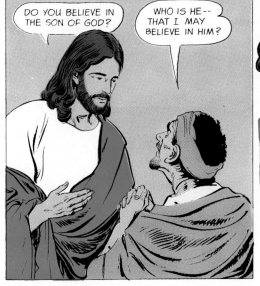

I AM THE GOOD SHEPHERD; THE GOOD SHEPHERD GIVES HIS LIFE FOR HIS SHEEP. NO ONE CAN TAKE MY LIFE FROM ME, BUT I GIVE IT MYSELF. I HAVE THE POWER TO GIVE IT AND TO TAKE IT AGAIN, FOR I RECEIVED THIS POWER FROM GOD MY FATHER.

THIS MAN IS CRAZY AND IS POSSESSED BY AN EVIL SPIRIT. WHY LISTEN TO HIM?

BUT CAN AN EVIL SPIRIT OPEN THE EYES OF THE BLIND?

WHILE JESUS IS PREACHING IN ONE OF THE CITIES A LAWYER IN THE CROWD WAITS FOR A CHANCE TO TEST HIM.

THE PHARISEES AND PRIESTS CONTINUE TO ARGUE. SOME THINK THAT JESUS IS WORKING WITH THE DEVIL. OTHERS DECLARE THAT HE IS NOT, BUT THEY REFUSE TO BELIEVE THAT HE IS THE SON OF GOD. A FEW DAYS LATER JESUS AND HIS DISCIPLES LEAVE JERUSALEM FOR A TOUR THROUGH JUDEA.

I'LL FIND OUT FOR MYSELF HOW THIS YOUNG TEACHER HANDLES A HARD QUESTION.

# Four Travelers to Jericho

FROM LUKE 10: 25-39

ONE DAY WHILE JESUS IS PREACHING A LAWYER DECIDES TO TEST HIM. HE ASKS A QUESTION WHICH THE PHARISEES HAVE ANSWERED WITH A LOT OF COMPLICATED RULES.

WHAT SHALL I DO TO INHERIT ETERNAL LIFE?

JESUS REPLIES BY ASKING A QUESTION THAT FORCES THE LAWYER TO DISREGARD THE RULES OF THE PHARISEES AND GO STRAIGHT TO THE COMMANDMENTS OF GOD.

YOU ARE AN AUTHORITY ON GOD'S WORD -- WHAT DO HIS COMMANDMENTS SAY?

LOVE GOD WITH ALL THY HEART -- AND THY NEIGHBOR AS THYSELF.

YOU ARE RIGHT-- DO THAT AND YOU WILL HAVE ETERNAL LIFE.

BUT WHO IS MY NEIGHBOR?

JESUS REPLIES WITH A STORY WHICH FORCES THE LAWYER AGAIN TO ANSWER HIS OWN QUESTION:

A MAN IS TRAVELING FROM JERUSALEM TO JERICHO. ON THE WAY HE IS ATTACKED BY BANDITS, ROBBED, AND LEFT FOR DEAD.

BY CHANCE A PRIEST COMES BY-- HE SEES THE WOUNDED MAN BUT HE QUICKLY PASSES BY.

A LITTLE LATER A LEVITE, AN ASSISTANT TO THE PRIESTS, COMES ALONG-- BUT HE, TOO, HURRIES BY.

BUT WHEN A SAMARITAN SEES THE INJURED MAN, HE STOPS. ALTHOUGH SAMARITANS ARE BITTER ENEMIES OF THE JEWS, HE BINDS UP THE MAN'S WOUNDS, TAKES HIM TO AN INN, AND PAYS FOR HIS CARE.

WHEN HE FINISHES THE STORY OF THE GOOD SAMARITAN, JESUS ASKS: WHICH ONE OF THE THREE WAS A NEIGHBOR TO THE MAN WHO WAS ROBBED?

THE MAN WHO HELPED HIM.

GO AND DO THE SAME.

THE LAWYER GOES AWAY-- AMAZED AT THE SKILL WITH WHICH JESUS ANSWERED HIS QUESTIONS.

NOW I SEE-- MY NEIGHBOR IS ANYONE WHO NEEDS ME.

JESUS CONTINUES ON HIS PREACHING TOUR. IN BETHANY HE STOPS TO VISIT HIS FRIENDS: MARY, MARTHA, AND LAZARUS. MARY DROPS EVERYTHING SHE IS DOING TO LISTEN TO JESUS...

BUT HER SISTER MARTHA...

IT ISN'T FAIR-- AND I WON'T STAND FOR IT ANY LONGER!

# The Lord's Prayer

FROM LUKE 10:40—11:2; MATTHEW 6:9-13;
JOHN 10:22-40; LUKE 15:1-19

WHEN JESUS VISITS IN THE HOME OF HIS FRIENDS, MARY, MARTHA, AND LAZARUS, MARY STOPS HER WORK TO LISTEN TO JESUS. BUT MARTHA HURRIES TO THE KITCHEN TO PREPARE FOOD. AS SHE WORKS SHE BECOMES UPSET BECAUSE MARY DOES NOT HELP HER. AT LAST SHE COMPLAINS TO JESUS.

DON'T YOU THINK IT'S WRONG FOR MARY TO LEAVE ME WITH ALL THE WORK TO DO? TELL HER TO HELP ME.

MARTHA! MARTHA! YOU ARE WORRYING ABOUT TOO MANY THINGS. ONLY ONE THING IS IMPORTANT --TO LEARN THE WILL OF GOD, AS MARY HAS CHOSEN TO DO.

DURING THE REST OF JESUS' VISIT, MARTHA SEEKS TO LEARN MORE ABOUT GOD. THEN JESUS LEAVES HIS FRIENDS IN BETHANY AND JOINS HIS DISCIPLES FOR A TEACHING TRIP IN JUDEA.

LISTENING TO JESUS MAKES ME FEEL SO CLOSE TO GOD.

DURING HIS TRAVELS JESUS STOPS OFTEN TO PRAY. HIS DISCIPLES SEE THE POWER OF PRAYER IN JESUS' LIFE, AND ONE DAY A DISCIPLE SPEAKS TO HIM ABOUT IT.

TEACH US TO PRAY.

JESUS ANSWERS: WHEN YOU PRAY, SAY,

OUR FATHER WHICH ART IN HEAVEN, HALLOWED BE THY NAME. THY KINGDOM COME. THY WILL BE DONE IN EARTH, AS IT IS IN HEAVEN. GIVE US THIS DAY OUR DAILY BREAD. AND FORGIVE US OUR DEBTS, AS WE FORGIVE OUR DEBTORS. AND LEAD US NOT INTO TEMPTATION, BUT DELIVER US FROM EVIL: FOR THINE IS THE KINGDOM, AND THE POWER, AND THE GLORY, FOR EVER. AMEN.

FOR A MOMENT NO ONE SPEAKS. THEN SOFTLY THE DISCIPLES SAY "AMEN" TO THE SIMPLE PRAYER THAT BECOMES A MODEL FOR THEIR FUTURE PRAYERS TO GOD. AFTER THIS, JESUS AND HIS HELPERS CONTINUE THROUGH JUDEA, PREACHING AND HEALING. BY THE TIME JESUS RETURNS TO JERUSALEM FOR A RELIGIOUS FEAST THE CITY IS FILLED WITH PEOPLE TALKING AND WONDERING ABOUT HIM.

AS JESUS IS WALKING ALONG SOLOMON'S PORCH OF THE TEMPLE, THE PEOPLE SURROUND HIM.

HOW LONG WILL YOU KEEP US WAITING? IF YOU ARE THE MESSIAH, TELL US.

I TOLD YOU, BUT YOU WOULD NOT BELIEVE ME. THE THINGS I HAVE DONE IN MY FATHER'S NAME SHOULD PROVE TO YOU WHO I AM.

DID YOU HEAR THAT? HE CALLED GOD HIS FATHER!

STONE HIM!

JESUS TURNS AND QUIETLY WALKS AWAY, AND--STRANGELY--NO ONE TRIES TO STOP HIM.

JESUS LEAVES JERUSALEM FOR PEREA--WHERE HE CONTINUES TO PREACH AND HEAL THE SICK. AGAIN THE PHARISEES COMPLAIN BECAUSE HE ASSOCIATES WITH SINNERS. JESUS TELLS THEM A STORY...

A CERTAIN MAN HAS TWO SONS. ONE DAY THE YOUNGER COMES TO HIM.

FATHER, I WANT TO RUN MY OWN LIFE. PLEASE GIVE ME THE SHARE OF YOUR MONEY THAT WILL SOMEDAY BE MINE.

I HAD HOPED YOU WOULD STAY HOME AND HELP WITH THE WORK HERE--BUT IF YOU WANT THE MONEY, YOU MAY HAVE IT.

THE YOUNG MAN GOES TO ANOTHER COUNTRY-- WHERE HE SPENDS HIS MONEY EATING AND DRINKING WITH BAD COMPANIONS. AT LAST HIS MONEY IS GONE--AND THE ONLY JOB HE CAN GET IS CARING FOR A FARMER'S PIGS.

MY FATHER'S SERVANTS LIVE BETTER THAN THIS! I'M GOING HOME AND ASK MY FATHER TO LET ME WORK FOR HIM--NOT AS HIS SON, BUT AS A SERVANT!

# The Prodigal's Return

FROM LUKE 15:20-32; JOHN 11:1-8

WHEN THE PHARISEES COMPLAIN BECAUSE JESUS ASSOCIATES WITH SINNERS, HE TELLS THEM A STORY ABOUT A YOUNG MAN WHO LEAVES HOME. THE YOUNG MAN SPENDS HIS MONEY SO FOOLISHLY THAT AT LAST HE HAS TO TAKE CARE OF A FARMER'S PIGS IN ORDER TO KEEP ALIVE. IN HIS MISERY HE DECIDES TO GO HOME AND WORK FOR HIS FATHER-- NOT AS HIS SON, BUT AS ONE OF HIS SERVANTS. WHEN HE REACHES HOME HIS FATHER RUSHES OUT TO MEET HIM.

FATHER! I HAVE SINNED AGAINST HEAVEN AND YOU. I'M NO LONGER WORTHY TO BE CALLED YOUR SON.

BRING MY SON THE BEST ROBE IN THE HOUSE. AND PREPARE A FEAST, FOR MY SON WHO WAS LOST IS FOUND!

OUT IN THE FIELD THE OLDER SON WORKS HARD TO COMPLETE HIS JOB BEFORE NIGHT.

IF MY BROTHER WERE HERE TO HELP, I WOULDN'T HAVE TO WORK SO MUCH.

THE DAY'S WORK DONE, HE GOES HOME. BUT AS HE APPROACHES THE HOUSE HE HEARS MUSIC...

WHAT'S GOING ON?

YOUR BROTHER HAS RETURNED, AND YOUR FATHER IS HAVING A FEAST FOR HIM.

IN ANGER THE OLDER SON REFUSES TO GO INTO THE HOUSE. SOON HIS FATHER COMES OUT.

YOU HAVE NEVER GIVEN A FEAST FOR ME ALTHOUGH I HAVE STAYED HOME TO HELP YOU. BUT MY BROTHER--

ALL THAT I HAVE IS YOURS, MY SON. BUT IT IS RIGHT FOR US TO BE GLAD FOR YOUR BROTHER'S RETURN. HE WAS THE SAME AS DEAD-- NOW HE IS ALIVE.

WHEN JESUS FINISHES THE STORY THE PEOPLE TURN TO ONE ANOTHER IN WONDER.

DOES HE MEAN THAT GOD IS LIKE THE FATHER IN THE STORY?

YES-- I SEE IT. GOD WANTS TO FORGIVE EVEN US SINNERS IF WE WILL COME BACK TO HIM.

WHEN THE PHARISEES SEE THE REACTION OF THE PEOPLE, THEY TURN AWAY IN ANGER. JESUS CONTINUES TO TEACH, BUT HE IS SOON INTERRUPTED...

JESUS! MARY AND MARTHA HAVE SENT ME TO TELL YOU THAT THEIR BROTHER, LAZARUS, IS ILL. THEY WANT YOU TO COME TO BETHANY--

BETHANY? THAT'S TOO CLOSE TO HIS ENEMIES IN JERUSALEM. THEY'LL KILL HIM!

# Called from the Tomb

JOHN 11: 38-54; LUKE 18: 15-23; 19:1-3

BY THE TIME JESUS AND HIS DISCIPLES REACH BETHANY LAZARUS, THE BROTHER OF MARY AND MARTHA, HAS BEEN DEAD FOUR DAYS. AT THE TOMB JESUS ASKS TO HAVE THE STONE ROLLED AWAY. HE PRAYS ALOUD TO GOD, AND THEN CALLS OUT IN A STRONG VOICE...

LAZARUS, COME FORTH.

TO THE AMAZEMENT OF THE CROWD, LAZARUS APPEARS!

LAZARUS!

O JESUS, WE THANK YOU!

A MAN RAISED FROM THE DEAD! THE PEOPLE CAN SCARCELY BELIEVE WHAT THEY HAVE SEEN. MANY OF THEM TURN TO JESUS CRYING, "MESSIAH! SON OF GOD!" BUT OTHERS GO INTO JERUSALEM TO TELL THE PHARISEES WHAT JESUS HAS DONE.

IN ANGER AND DESPERATION THE PHARISEES AND CHIEF PRIESTS CALL A MEETING.

IF NEWS OF THIS GETS AROUND THE PEOPLE WILL TRY TO MAKE JESUS A KING.

AND IF THERE'S A REBELLION THE ROMANS WILL BLAME **US**. WE'LL LOSE OUR POSITIONS AND THE NATION WILL BE DESTROYED.

84

FARTHER ALONG THE WAY JESUS IS STOPPED BY A YOUNG MAN.

TEACHER, WHAT SHALL I DO TO INHERIT ETERNAL LIFE?

KEEP GOD'S COMMANDMENTS.

BUT I HAVE KEPT THE LAWS --SINCE I WAS A BOY.

YOU NEED TO DO ONE THING MORE --SELL ALL THAT YOU HAVE, GIVE THE MONEY TO THE POOR, AND FOLLOW ME.

BUT THE YOUNG MAN THINKS TOO MUCH OF HIS RICHES...SLOWLY HE TURNS HIS BACK ON JESUS AND WALKS AWAY.

THE TRAVELERS CONTINUE ON TOWARD JERUSALEM. BY THE TIME THEY REACH JERICHO, JESUS IS IN THE MIDST OF AN EXCITED, HAPPY THRONG.

PLEASE --LET ME THROUGH!

HO--ZACCHEUS, THE CROOKED LITTLE TAX COLLECTOR, WANTS TO SEE JESUS!

I HAVE TO SEE JESUS--AND I WILL!

# Man in the Tree
LUKE 19:4-10; JOHN 12:1-8; LUKE 19:29-35

ZACCHEUS, THE WEALTHY TAX COLLECTOR,
IS SO SHORT THAT HE CAN'T LOOK
OVER THE HEADS OF THE PEOPLE. FRANTICALLY
HE RUNS AHEAD OF THE CROWD, CLIMBS A TREE,
AND WAITS. WHEN JESUS
SEES HIM, HE STOPS...

86

ZACCHEUS IS AMAZED THAT JESUS WOULD EVEN SPEAK TO HIM, BUT HE CLIMBS DOWN AT ONCE AND LEADS THE WAY TO HIS HOUSE.

WHY WOULD A TEACHER AS GREAT AS JESUS WANT TO STAY WITH THAT CROOKED LITTLE TAX COLLECTOR?

ZACCHEUS WONDERS, TOO, BUT HE SOON DISCOVERS THAT BEING IN THE PRESENCE OF JESUS MAKES HIM ASHAMED OF EVERY WRONG THING HE HAS EVER DONE. HE WANTS TO BE FORGIVEN AND START OVER...

HALF OF MY GOODS I WILL GIVE TO THE POOR. AND IF I HAVE CHEATED ANYONE I WILL PAY HIM BACK FOUR TIMES AS MUCH.

SALVATION HAS COME TO YOU TODAY, ZACCHEUS. IT IS TO HELP PEOPLE LIKE YOU THAT I HAVE COME TO THE WORLD.

FROM JERICHO THE CROWDS CONTINUE THEIR WAY TO JERUSALEM FOR THE GREAT PASSOVER FEAST. THE FESTIVAL IS STILL SIX DAYS AWAY, SO JESUS STOPS IN BETHANY TO VISIT HIS FRIENDS -- MARY, MARTHA, AND LAZARUS. AT A SUPPER IN THE HOME OF SIMON THE LEPER, MARY KNEELS BESIDE JESUS AND ANOINTS HIS FEET WITH COSTLY OIL -- THEN WIPES THEM WITH HER HAIR.

JUDAS ISCARIOT, TREASURER OF THE DISCIPLES, IS ANGERED BY WHAT HE THINKS IS A WASTE OF MONEY.

WHY WASN'T THE OIL SOLD AND THE MONEY GIVEN TO THE POOR?

I WANTED TO HONOR JESUS--

LET HER ALONE. SHE IS SHOWING HER LOVE FOR ME.

JUDAS IS ANGERED BY THIS REPRIMAND-- AND AN UGLY THOUGHT COMES TO HIS MIND.

WHEN THE TIME IS RIGHT I'LL GO TO THE PRIESTS AND PHARISEES-- **THEY'LL** BE GLAD TO LISTEN TO ME.

THE NEXT DAY JESUS AND HIS DISCIPLES JOIN THE CROWDS GOING UP TO JERUSALEM TO PREPARE FOR THE PASSOVER FEAST. ON THE WAY...

GO OVER INTO THAT VILLAGE AND AS YOU ENTER YOU WILL FIND A COLT. BRING IT TO ME. AND IF ANYONE QUESTIONS YOU, TELL HIM I NEED THE ANIMAL-- AND WILL RETURN IT.

PUZZLED, THE TWO DISCIPLES GO TO THE VILLAGE WHERE THEY FIND THE COLT. WHEN THEY START TO UNTIE THE ROPE...

WHAT DO YOU MEAN, TAKING MY ANIMAL?

JESUS SAID TO TELL YOU THAT HE NEEDED IT.

AT THE MENTION OF JESUS' NAME, THE MAN GLADLY GIVES HIS CONSENT.

I WONDER WHY JESUS WANTS MY COLT. IT HAS NEVER BEEN RIDDEN-- BESIDES, IT'S NOT A VERY NOBLE BEAST FOR ANYONE AS IMPORTANT AS JESUS TO RIDE.

# Triumphal Entry

LUKE 19: 36-38; MATTHEW 21: 10-17.

IT IS THE FIRST DAY OF THE WEEK. THE ROAD TO JERUSALEM IS FILLED WITH PEOPLE ON THE WAY TO CELEBRATE THE PASSOVER FEAST OF THE JEWS. AT JESUS' REQUEST HIS DISCIPLES BRING HIM A LOWLY BEAST OF BURDEN -- HE MOUNTS IT AND JOINS THE MULTITUDE OF PILGRIMS. EAGERLY THEY MAKE WAY FOR HIM -- WAVING PALM BRANCHES AND CARPETING HIS PATH WITH THEIR GARMENTS. AND, WHILE THEY ESCORT HIM -- TRIUMPHANTLY -- UP THE ROAD AND INTO THE CITY, THE SOUND OF THEIR PRAISES FILLS THE AIR: "HOSANNA! BLESSED IS THE KING THAT COMETH IN THE NAME OF THE LORD!"

90

THE CHILDREN'S PRAISE ANGERS THE PRIESTS AND PHARISEES.

DO YOU HEAR WHAT THEY ARE SAYING?

YES, AND HAVE YOU NOT READ IN THE PSALMS THAT OUT OF THE MOUTHS OF CHILDREN GOD BRINGS PERFECT PRAISE?

THAT EVENING JESUS GOES BACK TO BETHANY, BUT ON MONDAY WHEN HE RETURNS TO THE TEMPLE IN JERUSALEM...

I HAVE COME A LONG WAY TO OFFER A SACRIFICE TO GOD, BUT I CAN'T PAY SUCH A HIGH PRICE FOR THE DOVES.

SOMEONE ELSE WILL-- SO MOVE ON.

IN RIGHTEOUS ANGER JESUS DRIVES THE MERCHANTS OUT OF THE TEMPLE.

IS IT NOT WRITTEN IN THE SCRIPTURES THAT "MY HOUSE SHALL BE CALLED A HOUSE OF PRAYER"? BUT YOU HAVE MADE IT A DEN OF THIEVES.

WHEN JESUS BEGINS TO PREACH, PEOPLE CROWD INTO THE TEMPLE COURTS TO HEAR HIM. BUT BEHIND CLOSED DOORS THE PRIESTS AND PHARISEES PLOT THEIR STRATEGY. BY TUESDAY THEY ARE READY...

# The Great Commandment

LUKE 20: 23-26; MARK 12: 28-34, 38-44; 13;
MATTHEW 26: 14-16

JESUS IS PREACHING IN A COURT OF THE TEMPLE, AND IN AN ATTEMPT TO GET HIM INTO TROUBLE, THE PHARISEES ASK: "IS IT RIGHT TO PAY TAXES TO CAESAR?" JESUS KNOWS THAT THIS IS A TRICK QUESTION. IF HE ANSWERS "YES," THE PEOPLE WILL TURN AGAINST HIM. IF HE SAYS "NO," THE ROMANS WILL ARREST HIM FOR TREASON. HE ASKS TO SEE A ROMAN COIN.

WHOSE IMAGE IS THIS?

CAESAR'S.

QUIETLY JESUS RETURNS THE COIN.

GIVE TO CAESAR THE THINGS THAT ARE HIS, AND TO GOD THE THINGS THAT ARE GOD'S.

THE PHARISEES ARE ANGRY AT BEING DEFEATED AGAIN, BUT THEY MARVEL AT JESUS' SKILL IN HANDLING THEIR TRICK QUESTION. LATER IN THE DAY ONE OF THEM ASKS ANOTHER DIFFICULT QUESTION.

WHICH OF OUR 613 COMMANDMENTS IS THE MOST IMPORTANT?

THOU SHALT LOVE THE LORD THY GOD WITH ALL THY HEART, AND WITH ALL THY SOUL, AND WITH ALL THY MIND, AND WITH ALL THY STRENGTH. AND THE SECOND IS THIS: THOU SHALT LOVE THY NEIGHBOR AS THYSELF.

YOU HAVE SPOKEN THE TRUTH. TO LOVE GOD AND ONE'S NEIGHBOR IS MORE IMPORTANT THAN ALL BURNT OFFERINGS.

YOU ARE NOT FAR FROM THE KINGDOM OF GOD.

94

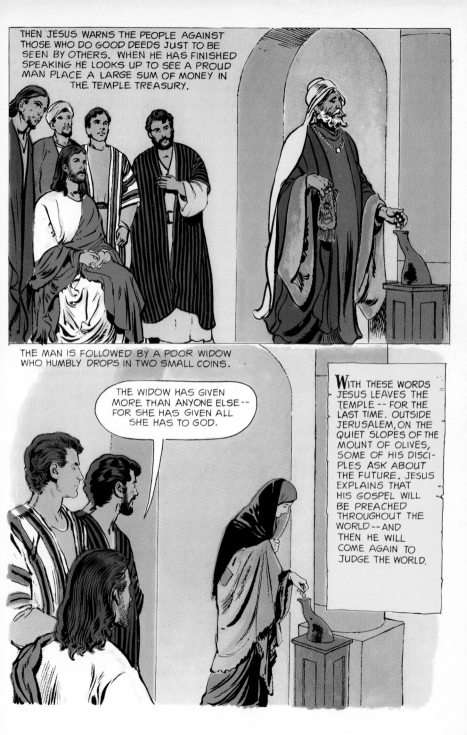

THEN JESUS WARNS THE PEOPLE AGAINST THOSE WHO DO GOOD DEEDS JUST TO BE SEEN BY OTHERS. WHEN HE HAS FINISHED SPEAKING HE LOOKS UP TO SEE A PROUD MAN PLACE A LARGE SUM OF MONEY IN THE TEMPLE TREASURY.

THE MAN IS FOLLOWED BY A POOR WIDOW WHO HUMBLY DROPS IN TWO SMALL COINS.

THE WIDOW HAS GIVEN MORE THAN ANYONE ELSE -- FOR SHE HAS GIVEN ALL SHE HAS TO GOD.

WITH THESE WORDS JESUS LEAVES THE TEMPLE -- FOR THE LAST TIME. OUTSIDE JERUSALEM, ON THE QUIET SLOPES OF THE MOUNT OF OLIVES, SOME OF HIS DISCIPLES ASK ABOUT THE FUTURE. JESUS EXPLAINS THAT HIS GOSPEL WILL BE PREACHED THROUGHOUT THE WORLD -- AND THEN HE WILL COME AGAIN TO JUDGE THE WORLD.

# Secretly—in an Upper Room

LUKE 22:7-13; JOHN 13:1-20, 27-30;
MATTHEW 26:21-25

IT IS LATE TUESDAY NIGHT WHEN JUDAS BARGAINS WITH THE CHIEF PRIESTS TO BETRAY JESUS. AFTER THE AGREEMENT IS MADE HE RETURNS TO BETHANY AND SPENDS WEDNESDAY WITH JESUS AND THE DISCIPLES-- NEVER SUSPECTING THAT JESUS KNOWS WHAT HE HAS DONE. THURSDAY, JESUS CALLS PETER AND JOHN ASIDE.

GO INTO JERUSALEM AND MAKE THINGS READY FOR THE PASSOVER FEAST.

WHERE CAN WE GO SO THAT YOUR ENEMIES WILL NOT SEE US?

WHEN YOU ENTER THE CITY YOU WILL SEE A MAN CARRYING A PITCHER. FOLLOW HIM AND ASK HIS MASTER TO SHOW YOU THE ROOM THAT WE MAY USE.

PETER AND JOHN GO AT ONCE TO JERUSALEM. THEY FIND THE SERVANT CARRYING A PITCHER AND FOLLOW HIM HOME.

WHERE IS THE ROOM IN WHICH JESUS AND HIS DISCIPLES CAN EAT THE PASSOVER?

COME WITH ME.

THE MAN LEADS THEM QUICKLY UP THE STAIRS TO A BIG UPPER ROOM.

I'M HONORED TO HAVE JESUS CELEBRATE THE PASSOVER IN MY HOUSE.

PETER AND JOHN PREPARE FOR THE FEAST, AND THAT EVENING JESUS JOINS THE TWELVE IN THE UPPER ROOM. AFTER THEY ARE SEATED JESUS KNEELS, LIKE A SERVANT, TO WASH THE FEET OF HIS DISCIPLES.

NO, LORD. I'M NOT GOOD ENOUGH TO HAVE **YOU** WAIT ON ME!

IF YOU DO NOT LET ME SERVE YOU, PETER, YOU WILL HAVE NO PLACE IN MY KINGDOM.

AFTER JESUS HAS WASHED ALL OF THE DISCIPLES' FEET, HE SITS DOWN AT THE TABLE AGAIN.

IF I, YOUR LORD AND MASTER, HAVE SERVED YOU, YOU SHOULD DO THE SAME FOR ONE ANOTHER. THE SERVANT IS NOT GREATER THAN HIS MASTER.

AFTER A FEW MINUTES JESUS MAKES A STARTLING STATEMENT.

ONE OF YOU IS GOING TO BETRAY ME.

BETRAY YOU? IS IT I, LORD?

JESUS REPLIES THAT IT IS ONE WHO IS EATING WITH HIM NOW. JUDAS LEANS FORWARD.

IS IT I?

YOU HAVE SAID IT. WHAT YOU ARE GOING TO DO, JUDAS, DO QUICKLY.

AT ONCE THE TRAITOR RISES FROM THE TABLE AND HURRIES AWAY. BUT THE OTHER DISCIPLES DO NOT UNDERSTAND WHY..

# The Lord's Supper

LUKE 22:17-20; JOHN 13:33-38; 14;
MATTHEW 26:30, 36-56

AFTER JUDAS, THE TRAITOR, LEAVES,
JESUS PICKS UP A PIECE OF BREAD,
THANKS GOD FOR IT, BREAKS IT,
AND GIVES IT TO HIS DISCIPLES,
SAYING, "THIS IS MY BODY."
WHEN THEY HAVE EATEN THE
BREAD, HE OFFERS THEM
A CUP.

DRINK OF IT, EACH ONE
OF YOU, FOR IT IS MY
BLOOD, WHICH WILL BE
SHED TO PAY THE PRICE OF
YOUR SINS. AFTER I'M
GONE, DO THIS IN
REMEMBRANCE OF ME.

THUS JESUS MAKES A NEW
COVENANT BETWEEN GOD
AND MEN. AS MEN TAKE THE
BREAD AND WINE IN THE NAME
OF JESUS THEY ARE REMINDED
THAT GOD, THROUGH HIS SON,
HAS DELIVERED THEM FROM THE
SLAVERY OF SIN.

IN A LITTLE WHILE I MUST LEAVE YOU. YOU CANNOT FOLLOW ME, BUT BEFORE I GO, LET ME REMIND YOU: LOVE ONE ANOTHER AS I HAVE LOVED YOU.

LORD, WHY CAN'T I FOLLOW YOU? YOU KNOW I'D GIVE MY LIFE FOR YOU.

PETER, BEFORE THE COCK CROWS YOU WILL DENY ME THREE TIMES.

DENY MY LORD? NEVER! MY SWORD IS READY THIS MINUTE FOR THE FIRST PERSON WHO TRIES TO HARM HIM.

THE DISCIPLES ARE FRIGHTENED AT THE THOUGHT OF JESUS LEAVING THEM.

DO NOT BE AFRAID. BELIEVE IN GOD; BELIEVE ALSO IN ME. IF YOU LOVE ME, KEEP MY COMMANDMENTS. AND I WILL ASK GOD TO SEND YOU THE HOLY SPIRIT TO COMFORT YOU. HE WILL BE WITH YOU FOREVER. COME, IT IS TIME TO GO...

QUIETLY, THEY LEAVE THE UPPER ROOM. THEY WALK THROUGH THE MOONLIT STREETS OF THE CITY, OUT AN EAST GATE, AND ACROSS A VALLEY TO THE GARDEN OF GETHSEMANE ON THE MOUNT OF OLIVES.

AT THE ENTRANCE JESUS ASKS EIGHT OF THE DISCIPLES TO WAIT WHILE HE TAKES HIS CLOSEST DISCIPLES, PETER, JAMES, AND JOHN FARTHER INTO THE GARDEN.

THIS IS A SAD NIGHT FOR ME -- STAY HERE AND WATCH WHILE I GO ALONE TO PRAY.

O MY FATHER, IF THOU BE WILLING, REMOVE THIS AGONY FROM ME; NEVERTHELESS, NOT MY WILL, BUT THINE BE DONE.

WHEN JESUS RETURNS TO HIS DISCIPLES, HE FINDS THEM SLEEPING. TWO MORE TIMES HE GOES ASIDE TO PRAY, AND EACH TIME HE FINDS HIS FRIENDS ASLEEP. AFTER WAKING THEM THE THIRD TIME...

ARISE -- THE ONE WHO IS TO BETRAY ME IS NEAR.

AS JESUS SPEAKS, JUDAS LEADS A BAND OF MEN INTO THE GARDEN. ACCORDING TO HIS AGREEMENT, HE IDENTIFIES JESUS WITH A KISS.

GREETINGS, MASTER!

AS THE SOLDIERS TAKE HOLD OF JESUS, PETER DRAWS HIS SWORD. SLASHING WILDLY, HE CUTS OFF THE EAR OF A SERVANT.

PETER, PUT UP YOUR SWORD. DO YOU THINK THAT I CANNOT CALL ON GOD TO SEND LEGIONS OF ANGELS TO PROTECT ME?

QUIETLY JESUS HEALS THE MAN'S EAR. WHEN THE DISCIPLES SEE THAT JESUS IS MAKING NO ATTEMPT TO SAVE HIMSELF, THEY RUN FOR THEIR LIVES. AT AN OFFICER'S COMMAND, THE SOLDIERS BIND JESUS AND TAKE HIM BACK TO JERUSALEM -- THE CITY INTO WHICH HE HAD RIDDEN SO TRIUMPHANTLY ONLY A FEW DAYS BEFORE!

# Tried—and Denied!

MATTHEW 26:57-75; JOHN 18:28-38; LUKE 23:6-12

FOLLOWING HIS ARREST, JESUS IS BROUGHT TO THE PALACE OF THE HIGH PRIEST. FALSE WITNESSES BOLDLY ACCUSE HIM OF MANY THINGS --BUT THEY CAN PROVE NOTHING. FINALLY THE HIGH PRIEST QUESTIONS THE PRISONER.

ARE YOU THE CHRIST, THE SON OF GOD?

I AM.

THERE! YOU HEARD HIM. ANYONE WHO SPEAKS BLASPHEMY BY CLAIMING TO BE GOD'S SON DESERVES TO DIE.

INSTANTLY THE GUARDS TURN ON JESUS -- SPITTING ON HIM, COVERING HIS FACE AND DEMANDING THAT HE PROVE HIS POWER BY IDENTIFYING THOSE WHO STRIKE HIM.

WHILE JESUS IS SUFFERING THESE INSULTS, PETER -- WHO HAS SECRETLY FOLLOWED HIM INTO THE CITY -- WARMS HIS HANDS BY A FIRE IN THE PALACE COURTYARD. WHILE HE IS TALKING, A MAID STOPS AND LOOKS AT HIM...

YOU WERE ONE OF THOSE WITH JESUS OF NAZARETH.

ME? I DON'T KNOW WHAT YOU'RE TALKING ABOUT.

AFRAID OF BEING QUESTIONED FURTHER, PETER GOES OUT INTO THE HALLWAY, BUT THERE...

THIS FELLOW WAS WITH JESUS.

JESUS? I DON'T EVEN KNOW THE MAN.

ABOUT AN HOUR LATER SOME MEN APPROACH PETER.

DIDN'T I SEE YOU IN THE GARDEN WHEN THE SOLDIERS TOOK JESUS?

YOU ARE A GALILEAN LIKE JESUS. I CAN TELL BY THE WAY YOU TALK.

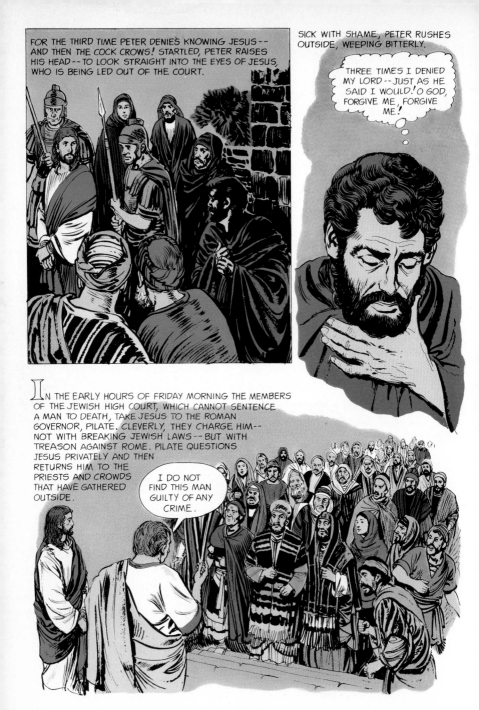

FOR THE THIRD TIME PETER DENIES KNOWING JESUS --
AND THEN THE COCK CROWS! STARTLED, PETER RAISES
HIS HEAD -- TO LOOK STRAIGHT INTO THE EYES OF JESUS,
WHO IS BEING LED OUT OF THE COURT.

SICK WITH SHAME, PETER RUSHES
OUTSIDE, WEEPING BITTERLY.

THREE TIMES I DENIED
MY LORD -- JUST AS HE
SAID I WOULD! O GOD,
FORGIVE ME, FORGIVE
ME!

IN THE EARLY HOURS OF FRIDAY MORNING THE MEMBERS
OF THE JEWISH HIGH COURT, WHICH CANNOT SENTENCE
A MAN TO DEATH, TAKE JESUS TO THE ROMAN
GOVERNOR, PILATE. CLEVERLY, THEY CHARGE HIM --
NOT WITH BREAKING JEWISH LAWS -- BUT WITH
TREASON AGAINST ROME. PILATE QUESTIONS
JESUS PRIVATELY AND THEN
RETURNS HIM TO THE
PRIESTS AND CROWDS
THAT HAVE GATHERED
OUTSIDE.

I DO NOT
FIND THIS MAN
GUILTY OF ANY
CRIME.

NOT GUILTY? WHY, HE TRIED TO START REVOLTS ALL OVER JUDEA AND GALILEE!

AT THE MENTION OF GALILEE, PILATE SENDS JESUS TO HEROD, THE RULER OF GALILEE, WHO IS IN JERUSALEM FOR THE PASSOVER. HEROD IS CURIOUS AND ASKS JESUS TO PERFORM SOME MIRACLE. WHEN JESUS WILL NOT, HEROD AND HIS SOLDIERS MAKE FUN OF HIM -- AND THEN RETURN HIM TO PILATE.

PILATE IS TRAPPED. HE DOES NOT BELIEVE JESUS IS GUILTY OF TREASON. "BUT, IF I LET HIM GO," HE ARGUES TO HIMSELF, "AND THE JEWISH LEADERS MAKE TROUBLE, THE EMPEROR IN ROME WILL HOLD ME RESPONSIBLE." FINALLY HE THINKS OF A WAY TO EASE HIS CONSCIENCE AND PROTECT HIMSELF...

THE PEOPLE! I'LL LET THEM DECIDE!

# Condemned to Die

JOHN 18:39—19:16; MATTHEW 27:3-10

THE JEWISH LEADERS HAVE CHARGED JESUS WITH TREASON AGAINST ROME. PILATE, THE ROMAN GOVERNOR, DOES NOT BELIEVE HE IS GUILTY--BUT HE IS AFRAID TO ANGER THE JEWS FOR FEAR THEY WILL STIR UP SO MUCH TROUBLE THAT THE REPORTS OF IT WILL REACH THE EMPEROR IN ROME. LOOKING AT THE CROWDS IN JERUSALEM FOR THE PASSOVER, HE SUDDENLY SEES A WAY OUT: LET THE PEOPLE DECIDE WHETHER OR NOT JESUS SHOULD DIE. BUT HE DOES NOT KNOW THAT THE PRIESTS ARE STIRRING UP THE CROWDS AGAINST JESUS.

IT IS THE CUSTOM TO RELEASE A PRISONER TO YOU DURING THE PASSOVER. WHICH SHALL I GIVE YOU-- JESUS, WHO IS CALLED THE CHRIST-- OR BARABBAS, THE MURDERER?

BARABBAS! GIVE US BARABBAS!

PILATE IS STUNNED. HE MAKES ANOTHER ATTEMPT TO SAVE JESUS.

SCOURGE HIM.

MAYBE THE PEOPLE WILL BE SATISFIED IF THE PRISONER IS PUNISHED.

SO JESUS IS WHIPPED WITH LEATHER THONGS. THEN, IN SPORT, THE SOLDIERS MAKE A CROWN OF THORNS AND PLACE IT ON HIS HEAD.

HAIL, THE KING OF THE JEWS!

HOPING THE SIGHT OF JESUS, BRUTALLY BEATEN, WILL AROUSE THE CROWD'S SYMPATHY, PILATE PRESENTS HIM TO THE MULTITUDE.

BEHOLD THE MAN!

CRUCIFY HIM!

CRUCIFY HIM!

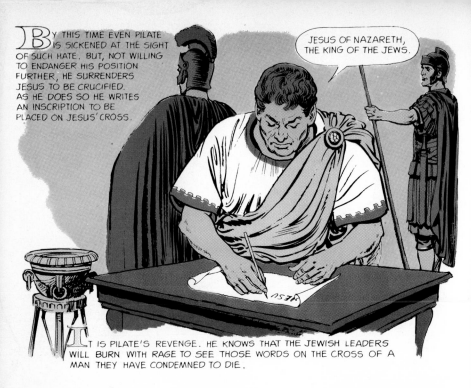

By this time even Pilate is sickened at the sight of such hate. But, not willing to endanger his position further, he surrenders Jesus to be crucified. As he does so he writes an inscription to be placed on Jesus' cross.

JESUS OF NAZARETH, THE KING OF THE JEWS.

It is Pilate's revenge. He knows that the Jewish leaders will burn with rage to see those words on the cross of a man they have condemned to die.

NO! NO! DON'T WRITE THAT HE IS THE KING OF THE JEWS. WRITE THAT HE SAID, "I AM KING OF THE JEWS."

WHAT I HAVE WRITTEN, I HAVE WRITTEN.

To Jesus, the hours from the time he was arrested until he is sentenced to be crucified have been filled with agony.

Sometime during those dark hours the traitor, Judas, realizes what he has done and rushes to the chief priests...

111

# A King Is Crucified

LUKE 23: 26-46; JOHN 19: 25-27

HAPPY, EXCITED PILGRIMS FROM ALL OVER PALESTINE HAVE BEEN CROWDING INTO JERUSALEM FOR DAYS TO CELEBRATE THE PASSOVER FEAST. BUT ON FRIDAY MORNING STARTLING NEWS SWEEPS ACROSS THE CITY LIKE A CHILLING WIND: JESUS OF NAZARETH IS GOING TO BE CRUCIFIED -- FOR TREASON!

THE STREET THAT LEADS TO THE HILL OF EXECUTION IS SOON FILLED WITH A STRANGE MIXTURE OF PEOPLE-- PRIESTS AND PHARISEES WHO DEMAND JESUS' DEATH; WOMEN WEEPING FOR THE MAN WHO FORGAVE SINS AND HEALED THE SICK; AND THE CURIOUS WHO WANT ONLY TO SEE A CONDEMNED MAN CARRY HIS CROSS...

ON THE WAY JESUS FALLS UNDER THE WEIGHT OF THE HEAVY CROSS. TO KEEP THE UGLY PROCESSION MOVING, THE ROMAN OFFICER SEIZES A BYSTANDER, SIMON FROM CYRENE.

HERE-- YOU CARRY THIS CROSS!

IT IS ABOUT NINE O'CLOCK WHEN JESUS, AND TWO ROBBERS WHO ARE TO BE CRUCIFIED WITH HIM, REACH CALVARY. AND THERE THE SON OF GOD IS NAILED TO A CROSS. ABOVE HIS HEAD IS FASTENED A SIGN: JESUS OF NAZARETH, THE KING OF THE JEWS!

FATHER, FORGIVE THEM: FOR THEY KNOW NOT WHAT THEY DO.

But to the Roman soldiers he is only another criminal being put to death according to Roman law.

THIS ROBE IS SEAMLESS -- HOW SHALL WE DIVIDE IT?

IT'S TOO GOOD TO TEAR INTO PIECES. LET'S CAST LOTS FOR IT.

As Jesus' friends stand watching, curious crowds pass by. Those who schemed for his death taunt him.

IF YOU'RE THE KING OF ISRAEL, COME DOWN FROM THE CROSS. THEN WE'LL BELIEVE YOU.

IF YOU'RE THE CHRIST, SAVE YOURSELF **AND** US.

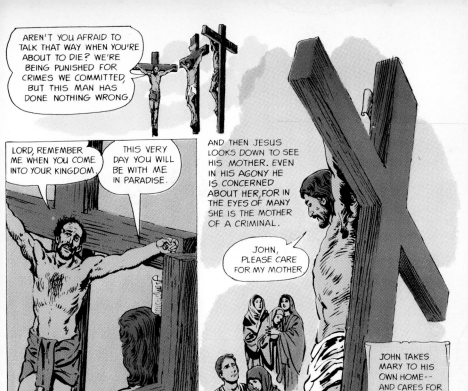

IT IS NOW NOON. SLOWLY, A STRANGE SHADOW COVERS THE LAND. FOR THREE HOURS THERE IS DARKNESS, THEN JESUS CRIES OUT TO GOD...

FATHER, INTO THY HANDS I COMMIT MY SPIRIT.

AND HAVING DONE SO, HE DIES. THE EARTH TREMBLES, AND IN JERUSALEM...

# The Sealed Tomb

MARK 15:38, 39; LUKE 23:48, 49;
JOHN 19:38-42; MATTHEW 27:62-66

AT ABOUT NINE O'CLOCK FRIDAY MORNING JESUS OF NAZARETH IS CRUCIFIED OUTSIDE THE WALLS OF JERUSALEM.

FROM NOON UNTIL THREE O'CLOCK DARKNESS COVERS THE LAND. THEN -- SUDDENLY -- AN EARTHQUAKE ROCKS THE GROUND. AND IN JERUSALEM...

THE VEIL BEFORE THE HOLIEST PLACE IN THE TEMPLE HAS BEEN RIPPED! WHAT CAN IT MEAN?

THE ANSWER IS THAT ON A HILL CALLED CALVARY THE SON OF GOD HAS GIVEN HIS LIFE TO PAY FOR THE SINS OF THE WORLD. THE VEIL IN THE TEMPLE NO LONGER SEPARATES MAN FROM THE PRESENCE OF GOD, FOR JESUS, THE SON, HAS OPENED THE WAY TO GOD, THE FATHER.

OUTSIDE THE CITY, EVEN THE ROMAN OFFICER WHO DIRECTED THE CRUCIFIXION IS AWED BY WHAT HAS HAPPENED. REVERENTLY, HE LOOKS UP AT THE MAN WHO FORGAVE HIS ENEMIES.

TRULY THIS MAN WAS GOD'S SON!

THE PEOPLE, TOO, ARE SHAKEN BY THE EXECUTION. AS THEY TURN BACK TO THE CITY...

I HAD HOPED THAT HE WAS THE ONE WHO WOULD DELIVER US FROM THE ROMANS.

IN JERUSALEM JOSEPH OF ARIMATHEA, A MEMBER OF THE JEWISH HIGH COURT AND SECRETLY A FOLLOWER OF JESUS, GOES BOLDLY TO PILATE.

MAY I HAVE THE BODY OF JESUS SO THAT WE MAY BURY IT BEFORE THE SABBATH?

YES... I'LL GIVE ORDERS TO MY OFFICER IN CHARGE.

REVERENTLY, JOSEPH TAKES THE BODY OF JESUS FROM THE CROSS. THEN HE AND HIS FRIEND, NICODEMUS, WRAP IT IN LINEN CLOTH, AND PLACE IT IN JOSEPH'S GARDEN TOMB.

EARLY THE NEXT DAY THE PRIESTS AND PHARISEES ALSO GO TO PILATE...

WE REMEMBER JESUS SAID THAT AFTER THREE DAYS HE WOULD RISE FROM THE DEAD. ORDER YOUR SOLDIERS TO SEAL AND GUARD THE TOMB SO THAT HIS DISCIPLES CAN'T STEAL THE BODY AND CLAIM THAT JESUS MADE GOOD ON HIS BOAST.

TAKE THE SOLDIERS YOU NEED AND SET UP A GUARD UNTIL AFTER THE THIRD DAY.

So THE TOMB IS SEALED, AND ROMAN SOLDIERS ARE PLACED ON GUARD.

THERE-- THAT'S THE LAST WE'LL HEAR OF THIS MAN WHO CALLED HIMSELF THE SON OF GOD!

# The Lord Is Risen

MARK 16:1-7; JOHN 20:2-18; MATTHEW 28:11-15;
LUKE 24:13-32

FRIDAY -- JUST OUTSIDE JERUSALEM -- JESUS OF NAZARETH IS CRUCIFIED AND BURIED. AT THE REQUEST OF THE PRIESTS AND PHARISEES, THE TOMB IS SEALED AND ROMAN SOLDIERS SET TO GUARD IT.

BUT ON THE MORNING OF THE THIRD DAY THE EARTH TREMBLES. AN ANGEL OF THE LORD DESCENDS -- AND ROLLS THE HEAVY STONE ASIDE. TERRIFIED, THE SOLDIERS FALL TO THE GROUND. WHEN THEY CAN GET TO THEIR FEET THEY RUSH BACK TO THE CITY.

THAT SAME MORNING MARY MAGDALENE AND OTHER FRIENDS OF JESUS HURRY TO THE TOMB WITH SPICES TO ANOINT HIS BODY. ON THE WAY, THEY WORRY ABOUT HOW THEY WILL GET THE STONE ROLLED AWAY. BUT WHEN THEY REACH THE GARDEN...

THE TOMB! IT IS OPEN!

BELIEVING THAT SOMEONE HAS STOLEN JESUS' BODY, MARY RUNS BACK TO JERUSALEM TO TELL PETER AND JOHN. BUT THE OTHERS ENTER THE TOMB-- TO FIND AN ANGEL SEATED THERE.

DON'T BE FRIGHTENED. JESUS IS RISEN. GO, TELL HIS DISCIPLES.

IN THE CITY PETER AND JOHN ARE SO STARTLED BY MARY'S NEWS THAT THEY RACE BACK AHEAD OF HER. WHEN THEY REACH THE TOMB --

ONLY HIS BURIAL CLOTHES. WHAT DO YOU MAKE OF IT?

THAT HE ROSE FROM THE DEAD-- AS HE SAID HE WOULD. OH, WHY DIDN'T WE BELIEVE HIM!

BY THE TIME MARY REACHES THE GARDEN THE OTHERS HAVE GONE. IN HER GRIEF SHE DOES NOT RECOGNIZE THE VOICE OF ONE WHO QUESTIONS HER.

WHY DO YOU WEEP?

IF YOU HAVE TAKEN JESUS' BODY, TELL ME WHERE YOU HAVE LAID IT.

FTLY JESUS SPEAKS HER NAME--
ARY!" SHE TURNS -- AND SEES HER
EN LORD.

MASTER!

BUT JESUS' FRIENDS ARE NOT THE ONLY ONES WHO ARE EXCITED ABOUT WHAT HAPPENED IN THE GARDEN. IN JERUSALEM THE ROMAN SOLDIERS REPORT TO THE PRIESTS AND PHARISEES. AFRAID OF WHAT MAY HAPPEN IF THE TRUTH IS KNOWN, THEY ACT QUICKLY.

HERE, TAKE THIS MONEY. TELL PEOPLE THAT JESUS' DISCIPLES STOLE HIS BODY.

WHILE THE SOLDIERS SPREAD THEIR LIE, JESUS JOINS TWO OF HIS DISCIPLES ON THE WAY TO EMMAUS. THEY TALK WITH HIM, BUT THEY DO NOT KNOW WHO HE IS.

THAT EVENING AS THEY DINE IN EMMAUS, JESUS BLESSES THE BREAD -- AND WHEN HE HANDS IT TO THEM THEY SUDDENLY RECOGNIZE HIM.

JESUS!

AND JUST AS SUDDENLY HE VANISHES FROM THEIR SIGHT!

# Behind Locked Doors

LUKE 24:33-43; JOHN 20:19—21:6

IT IS LATE SUNDAY NIGHT--THROUGHOUT JERUSALEM PEOPLE ARE STILL TALKING ABOUT THE STRANGE REPORT OF THE ROMAN SOLDIERS.

THEY SAY JESUS' DISCIPLES STOLE HIS BODY TO MAKE US BELIEVE HE ROSE FROM THE DEAD.

I WONDER WHAT THOSE BRAVE ROMAN GUARDS WERE DOING WHILE THE TOMB WAS ROBBED. AND WHAT DO THE DISCIPLES SAY?

BUT JESUS' FRIENDS HAVE ALSO HEARD THE SOLDIERS' REPORT. THEY ARE AFRAID THEY MAY BE ARRESTED, SO THEY LOCK THE DOORS IN THE UPPER ROOM WHERE ALL--BUT THOMAS--HAVE GATHERED. TWO FRIENDS FIND THEM THERE.

JESUS IS ALIVE! WE WERE ON OUR WAY TO EMMAUS WHEN A STRANGER JOINED US. WE ASKED HIM TO HAVE SUPPER WITH US. AND WHEN HE BLESSED THE BREAD AND GAVE IT TO US, WE KNEW--ALL AT ONCE--THAT THE STRANGER WAS JESUS. THEN HE DISAPPEARED.

122

A WEEK LATER THOMAS IS WITH THE DISCIPLES WHEN THEY MEET AGAIN BEHIND LOCKED DOORS. ONCE MORE JESUS APPEARS TO THEM.

THOMAS, TOUCH MY HANDS AND MY SIDE.

MY LORD AND MY GOD!

BECAUSE YOU HAVE SEEN, THOMAS, YOU BELIEVE. BLESSED ARE THOSE WHO HAVE NOT SEEN AND YET HAVE BELIEVED.

AGAIN JESUS DISAPPEARS FROM THEIR SIGHT.

OBEYING A COMMAND THAT JESUS HAD GIVEN THEM, THE DISCIPLES GO NORTH TO GALILEE. ONE EVENING THEY GO FISHING. THEY FISH ALL NIGHT BUT CATCH NOTHING. AT DAYBREAK THEY SEE THE FIGURE OF A MAN STANDING ON THE SHORE.

CAST YOUR NET ON THE RIGHT SIDE OF THE BOAT.

THEY OBEY—AND SUDDENLY THE NET IS SO FULL OF FISH THEY CANNOT PULL IT IN.

# The Last Command

JOHN 21:7-18; MATTHEW 28:16-20; LUKE 24:44-51

ALL NIGHT THE DISCIPLES OF JESUS FISH IN THE SEA OF GALILEE--AND CATCH NOTHING. AT DAYBREAK THEY SEE A MAN ON SHORE WHO TELLS THEM TO CAST THEIR NET ON THE RIGHT SIDE OF THE BOAT. THEY OBEY--AND SUDDENLY THE NET IS SO FULL THAT THE RUGGED FISHERMEN CANNOT DRAW IT UP. JOHN LOOKS AGAIN AT THE FIGURE ON THE SHORE...

LOOK, PETER, IT IS THE LORD!

PETER IS SO EAGER TO REACH JESUS THAT HE JUMPS INTO THE WATER AND SWIMS TO LAND. THE OTHERS BRING THE BOAT IN AND ANCHOR IT OFFSHORE.
AFTER THE NET IS PULLED IN, JESUS CALLS TO HIS HUNGRY DISCIPLES.

COME AND EAT.

126

FOLLOWING THIS, THE ELEVEN
DISCIPLES RETURN TO
JERUSALEM. THERE JESUS
MEETS WITH THEM AND
EXPLAINS HOW--BY HIS
DEATH AND RESURRECTION--
HE HAS FULFILLED GOD'S MISSION
FOR HIM TO BE THE SAVIOR OF
THE WORLD. HE CHARGES THEM
TO CARRY ON THE WORK.
"BUT 'WAIT IN JERUSALEM,"
HE ADDS, "UNTIL THE POWER
OF GOD'S HOLY SPIRIT
COMES UPON YOU."

ON THE FORTIETH DAY
AFTER HIS RESURRECTION,
JESUS TAKES HIS DISCIPLES
TO THE MOUNT OF OLIVES
NEAR BETHANY. AND WHILE
HE IS BLESSING THEM, HE
ASCENDS INTO HEAVEN.

# The Acts of the Apostles,

THE FIFTH BOOK OF THE NEW TESTAMENT, TELLS HOW JESUS' DISCIPLES OBEYED HIS COMMAND TO GO INTO ALL THE WORLD AND PREACH THE GOSPEL.

## Waiting For a Promise

ACTS 1:1-26

FORTY DAYS AFTER HIS RESURRECTION JESUS TAKES HIS ELEVEN DISCIPLES TO THE MOUNT OF OLIVES, NEAR BETHANY. WHILE HE IS GIVING THEM HIS FINAL BLESSING, HE IS LIFTED UP OUT OF THEIR SIGHT. IN AWE AND WONDER THEY STAND LOOKING UP INTO HEAVEN AS IF TO CATCH ONE MORE GLIMPSE OF THE MASTER THEY LOVE. SUDDENLY TWO ANGELS APPEAR.

YOU MEN OF GALILEE, WHY DO YOU STAND HERE LOOKING UP INTO HEAVEN? JESUS WILL COME AGAIN-- IN THE VERY WAY YOU HAVE SEEN HIM GO.

THE ANGELS DISAPPEAR, AND PETER TURNS TO THE OTHERS.

LET'S DO WHAT JESUS TOLD US TO DO--GO BACK TO JERUSALEM AND WAIT FOR THE POWER HE PROMISED TO SEND US BEFORE WE BEGIN HIS WORK.

SO THE DISCIPLES, WHO HAD ONCE FLED FOR FEAR OF BEING ARRESTED AS FRIENDS OF JESUS, RETURN TO THE CITY-- KNOWING THAT JESUS IS DEPENDING ON THEM TO CARRY ON THE WORK FOR WHICH HE WAS CRUCIFIED.

IN JERUSALEM THEY TAKE LODGING IN AN UPPER ROOM WHICH SOON BECOMES A MEETING PLACE FOR OTHER FOLLOWERS OF JESUS.

JUDAS, WHO BETRAYED OUR LORD, IS DEAD. WE SHOULD APPOINT SOMEONE TO TAKE HIS PLACE.

I NOMINATE BARSABAS.

MATTHIAS.

THE DISCIPLES ASK GOD'S GUIDANCE IN THE CHOICE THEY MAKE -- AND MATTHIAS IS NAMED.

THE LORD HAS BLESSED YOU, MATTHIAS.

FOR THE NEXT TEN DAYS THE DISCIPLES MEET TOGETHER IN PRAYER -- WAITING FOR THE COMING OF THE HOLY SPIRIT. AT THE SAME TIME FAITHFUL JEWS FROM ALL OVER PALESTINE, AND EVEN DISTANT COUNTRIES, CROWD INTO JERUSALEM TO CELEBRATE THE FEAST OF THANKSGIVING CALLED PENTECOST.

MANY OF THE PILGRIMS PASS BY THE PLACE CALLED CALVARY, AND ARE REMINDED OF JESUS' CRUCIFIXION.

ROMAN SOLDIERS SAY JESUS' DISCIPLES STOLE HIS BODY FROM THE TOMB AND CLAIM HE ROSE FROM THE DEAD AS HE PROPHESIED HE WOULD.

BUT I'VE ALSO HEARD THAT A LOT OF PEOPLE SAW JESUS -- ALIVE. I HOPE I CAN FIND SOMEONE IN JERUSALEM WHO DID.

I'M SEEKING THE TRUTH -- BUT IT WILL TAKE A SIGN FROM GOD TO MAKE ME BELIEVE THAT JESUS' DISCIPLES SPEAK IT.

# Like Tongues of Fire!

ACTS 2:1-38

*WAS JESUS RAISED FROM THE DEAD? OR DID HIS DISCIPLES STEAL HIS BODY FROM THE TOMB AND CLAIM THAT HE WAS?*

THESE QUESTIONS ARE STILL BEING ASKED AS JEWS COME TO JERUSALEM TO CELEBRATE THE HARVEST FEAST CALLED PENTECOST. JESUS' DISCIPLES KNOW THE TRUTH; BUT THEY ARE WAITING FOR POWER FROM GOD TO HELP THEM PREACH IT TO THE WORLD.

EARLY ON THE DAY OF PENTECOST 120 FOLLOWERS OF JESUS ARE GATHERED IN A SECRET ROOM, PRAYING. SUDDENLY THERE IS A SOUND LIKE A RUSHING, MIGHTY WIND, AND GOD'S PRESENCE FILLS THE ROOM. THEN, LIKE TONGUES OF FIRE, HIS SPIRIT RESTS ON EACH ONE.

IN THAT SACRED MOMENT JESUS' FOLLOWERS ARE FILLED WITH STRENGTH AND COURAGE THEY HAVE NEVER KNOWN. RUSHING OUT OF THE UPPER ROOM AND INTO THE STREET BELOW, THEY BEGIN TO PREACH -- EACH IN A DIFFERENT LANGUAGE AS THE SPIRIT OF GOD DIRECTS.

THE CROWDS LISTEN WITH AMAZEMENT. AS THE STORY OF THIS STRANGE EVENT SPREADS, IT REACHES TWO MEN WHO HAVE COME TO JERUSALEM SEEKING THE TRUTH ABOUT JESUS.

LET'S FIND THE DISCIPLES AND SEE FOR OURSELVES IF WHAT THE PEOPLE ARE SAYING IS TRUE.

THEY FIND THE DISCIPLES, AND AS THEY LISTEN...

IT IS TRUE! EVERYONE IN JERUSALEM -- EVEN THOSE MEN FROM ARABIA, EGYPT, ROME, CRETE -- CAN UNDER- STAND WHAT THE DISCIPLES SAY. HOW DO YOU EXPLAIN IT?

THEY'VE BEEN DRINKING TOO MUCH NEW WINE.

DRUNKEN MEN DO NOT SUDDENLY SPEAK IN FOREIGN LANGUAGES -- AND WITH SUCH WISDOM.

132

In answer to this insult, Peter speaks out for all the disciples.

WE ARE NOT DRUNK! WE ARE FILLED WITH THE HOLY SPIRIT AS THE PROPHET JOEL PROPHESIED. YOU MEN OF JERUSALEM, YOU CRUCIFIED JESUS, THE CHOSEN ONE OF GOD. BUT GOD RAISED HIM FROM THE DEAD, AND WE ARE WITNESSES TO THAT RESURRECTION!

This bold charge cuts deep into the hearts of the people, for they remember how they called for Jesus' crucifixion.

REPENT OF YOUR SINS, AND BE BAPTIZED IN THE NAME OF JESUS CHRIST. THEN YOU SHALL RECEIVE THE GIFT OF THE HOLY SPIRIT AS WE HAVE!

YOU SAID IT WOULD TAKE A SIGN FROM GOD TO CONVINCE YOU THAT JESUS' DISCIPLES SPEAK THE TRUTH. WHAT DO YOU SAY NOW?

# Three Thousand in a Day

ACTS 2:38—3:7

WHEN PETER BOLDLY TELLS THE PEOPLE IN JERUSALEM THAT THEY CONDEMNED GOD'S CHOSEN ONE TO DIE, THEY ASK, "WHAT CAN WE DO?" "REPENT AND BE BAPTIZED IN THE NAME OF THE ONE YOU CRUCIFIED," PETER REPLIES. ONE BY ONE THE PEOPLE CRY OUT...

O GOD, FORGIVE MY SINS, IN THE NAME OF YOUR SON, JESUS CHRIST, WHO CAME TO SAVE ME!

YOU SAID ONLY A SIGN FROM GOD COULD MAKE YOU BELIEVE JESUS' DISCIPLES SPOKE THE TRUTH--

YES, AND I HAVE SEEN THAT SIGN. I BELIEVE JESUS LIVES. I BELIEVE HE IS THE SON OF GOD AND THAT THROUGH HIM MY SINS CAN BE FORGIVEN. HOW GOOD GOD IS TO GIVE ME A CHANCE TO BEGIN A NEW LIFE -- WITH JESUS!

ONE AFTERNOON WHEN PETER AND JOHN GO TO THE TEMPLE FOR PRAYER THEY FIND A LAME MAN BEGGING AT THE BEAUTIFUL GATE.

HAVE MERCY-- A COIN FOR THE POOR.

LOOK AT US!

MAYBE **BOTH** OF THEM WILL GIVE ME SOMETHING...

I HAVE NO MONEY, BUT I'LL GIVE YOU WHAT I HAVE. IN THE NAME OF JESUS CHRIST, RISE UP AND WALK!

WALK? THE MAN WHO HAS NEVER TAKEN A STEP IN HIS LIFE CANNOT BELIEVE WHAT HE HAS HEARD. BUT AS PETER REACHES OUT HIS HAND TO HIM, THE MAN STRETCHES FORTH HIS OWN...

# Miracle at the Gate

ACTS 3:7—4:17

To THE LAME BEGGAR AT THE TEMPLE GATE, PETER HOLDS OUT HIS HAND AND SAYS, "IN THE NAME OF JESUS CHRIST, RISE UP AND WALK!" AT ONCE THE MAN FEELS STRENGTH COME INTO HIS LEGS AND ANKLES. HE LEAPS TO HIS FEET!

I CAN WALK! PRAISE GOD, I CAN WALK!

IN HIS EXCITEMENT THE MAN RUSHES INTO THE TEMPLE, LEAPING AND SHOUTING FOR JOY.

LOOK! ISN'T THAT THE LAME MAN WHO WAS AT THE GATE?

YES, BUT--

GRATEFULLY, THE MAN TURNS TO PETER AND JOHN. THE CROWDS GATHER AROUND -- EAGER TO KNOW WHAT HAS HAPPENED.

WHY DO YOU LOOK AT US AS THOUGH **WE** MADE THIS MAN WALK? THE HEALING POWER CAME FROM GOD, WHO HAS DONE THIS TO HONOR JESUS WHOM **YOU** CRUCIFIED, BUT GOD RAISED FROM THE DEAD.

SEEING THAT HE HAS THE ATTENTION OF THE CROWD, PETER CONTINUES...

REPENT, AND TURN TO GOD SO THAT YOUR SINS MAY BE WIPED OUT. PREPARE YOURSELVES, FOR CHRIST WILL COME AGAIN...

AT THE BACK OF THE CROWD THE PRIESTS LISTEN. THEY ARE ANGRY—AND THEIR ANGER INCREASES AS THEY WATCH THE GROWING INTEREST OF THE PEOPLE.

HE MUST BE STOPPED AT ONCE--OR HE'LL HAVE ALL OF JERUSALEM BELIEVING THAT JESUS ROSE FROM THE DEAD.

WITH THE HELP OF THE CAPTAIN OF THE TEMPLE GUARDS, THE PRIESTS PUSH THEIR WAY THROUGH THE CROWDS.

YOU ARE UNDER ARREST!

WITHOUT ANOTHER WORD, PETER AND JOHN ARE MARCHED AWAY TO PRISON-- BUT ALREADY FIVE THOUSAND MEN HAVE DECLARED THEIR BELIEF IN JESUS.

THE NEXT MORNING THEY ARE BROUGHT BEFORE THE SANHEDRIN, THE SAME JEWISH COURT THAT CONDEMNED JESUS TO DEATH. BESIDE THEM--PERFECTLY WELL-- STANDS THE MAN WHO HAD BEEN LAME FROM BIRTH.

BY WHAT POWER AND IN WHOSE NAME HAVE YOU HEALED THIS MAN?

FILLED WITH THE HOLY SPIRIT, PETER SPEAKS OUT COURAGEOUSLY.

LET IT BE KNOWN TO YOU, AND ALL THE PEOPLE OF ISRAEL -- THIS MAN WAS HEALED BY THE NAME OF JESUS CHRIST OF NAZARETH, WHOM **YOU** CRUCIFIED!

THE COURT, IS STUNNED. PETER AND JOHN ARE UNEDUCATED FISHERMEN, YET THEY SPEAK AND ACT WITH AUTHORITY AND POWER.

TAKE THEM AWAY --UNTIL WE CALL FOR THEM AGAIN.

THE MINUTE THE PRISONERS ARE OUT OF SIGHT, THE COURT HOLDS A MEETING.

EVERYONE KNOWS A MIRACLE HAS TAKEN PLACE. WE CANNOT DENY IT, BUT WE MUST KEEP THE NEWS FROM SPREADING. WHAT CAN WE DO?

TELL THESE "PREACHERS" THAT IF THEY SPEAK AGAIN IN THE NAME OF JESUS THEY WILL BE PUT TO DEATH AS HE WAS!

# The Pretenders

ACTS 4:18—5:18

PETER TELLS THE PEOPLE THAT HE HEALED THE LAME MAN IN THE NAME OF JESUS, WHOM THEY AND THEIR LEADERS CRUCIFIED AND WHOM GOD RAISED FROM THE DEAD. THIS ANGERS THE PRIESTS; THEY HAVE PETER AND JOHN ARRESTED AND BROUGHT BEFORE THE COURT. THE PRIESTS WANT TO PUNISH THE DISCIPLES BUT ARE AFRAID THIS WILL STIR THE CROWDS TO RIOT.

WE WILL RELEASE YOU THIS TIME, BUT DON'T EVER PREACH ABOUT JESUS AGAIN.

WHETHER IT IS RIGHT IN THE EYES OF GOD FOR US TO OBEY HIM OR YOU, YOU MUST DECIDE. BUT WE HAVE TO KEEP ON PREACHING WHAT WE HAVE SEEN AND HEARD.

SUCH BOLDNESS ANGERS THE PRIESTS EVEN MORE, BUT AFTER THREATENING THE DISCIPLES AGAIN, THEY LET THEM GO. PETER AND JOHN HURRY BACK TO THEIR FRIENDS WHO IMMEDIATELY JOIN THEM IN PRAYER.

O GOD, GIVE US COURAGE TO SPEAK THY WORD FEARLESSLY.

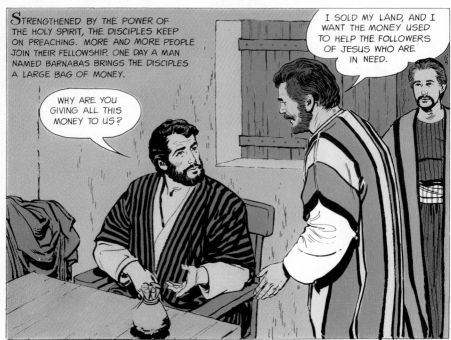

Strengthened by the power of the Holy Spirit, the disciples keep on preaching. More and more people join their fellowship. One day a man named Barnabas brings the disciples a large bag of money.

WHY ARE YOU GIVING ALL THIS MONEY TO US?

I SOLD MY LAND, AND I WANT THE MONEY USED TO HELP THE FOLLOWERS OF JESUS WHO ARE IN NEED.

142

THE PRAISE THAT IS SHOWERED ON BARNABAS FOR HIS GENEROUS GIFT PROMPTS A MAN NAMED ANANIAS AND HIS WIFE, SAPPHIRA, TO SEEK SUCH HONOR FOR THEMSELVES.

WE, TOO, HAVE SOLD OUR LAND AND WE WANT TO GIVE THE MONEY TO HELP THE CHURCH.

ANANIAS, THE MONEY WAS YOURS TO DO WITH AS YOU PLEASED. BUT WHY DO YOU PRETEND TO GIVE ALL, WHEN YOU KNOW THAT IS NOT TRUE? DON'T YOU SEE -- YOU ARE LYING TO GOD?

WHEN ANANIAS HEARS THESE WORDS, HE FALLS DOWN DEAD. SOME YOUNG MEN TAKE HIS BODY AWAY, AND AS THEY ARE RETURNING SAPPHIRA COMES IN. LIKE HER HUSBAND, SHE LIES ABOUT THE MONEY.

SAPPHIRA, YOUR HUSBAND IS DEAD BECAUSE HE LIED TO GOD. AND YOU WILL PAY THE SAME PENALTY.

INSTANTLY SAPPHIRA FALLS TO THE FLOOR -- AND DIES. THE FOLLOWERS OF JESUS LOOK ON THIS SEVERE PUNISHMENT AS A WARNING TO ANYONE WHO THINKS HE CAN PRETEND LOYALTY TO GOD.

IN SPITE OF THREATS, THE DISCIPLES KEEP ON HEALING IN THE NAME OF JESUS. THE PRIESTS WATCH--ANGRY BUT HELPLESS--AS FAMILIES BRING THEIR SICK ONES OUT INTO THE STREETS, WAITING FOR THE DISCIPLES TO PASS BY AND HEAL THEM.

HE IS LAME— PLEASE MAKE HIM STRONG SO THAT HE CAN RUN AND PLAY LIKE OTHER CHILDREN.

I CANNOT HEAL HIM, BUT JESUS, THE SON OF GOD, CAN. IN HIS NAME, I SAY TO YOU, YOUR SON IS HEALED.

THE FAME OF THE DISCIPLES SPREADS-- AND SOON PEOPLE FROM THE TOWNS ROUND ABOUT CROWD INTO JERUSALEM, BEGGING TO BE HEALED. AT LAST THE PRIESTS CAN STAND IT NO LONGER. IN A FIT OF RAGE THEY HAVE THE DISCIPLES ARRESTED AND THROWN INTO JAIL.

THIS TIME THERE WILL BE NO RELEASE!

# Missing Prisoners

ACTS 5:19—6:10

AFRAID THAT THE CROWDS MIGHT TURN AGAINST THEM, THE PRIESTS ARE FORCED TO STAND BY WHILE JESUS' DISCIPLES CONTINUE TO TEACH AND HEAL THE SICK. BUT WHEN PEOPLE FROM OTHER CITIES BEGIN TO POUR INTO JERUSALEM ASKING FOR THE DISCIPLES, THE PRIESTS CAN CONTROL THEIR JEALOUSY NO LONGER. THEY HAVE THE DISCIPLES ARRESTED AND THROWN INTO PRISON. DURING THE NIGHT AN ANGEL FROM GOD RELEASES THEM.

GO--STAND IN THE TEMPLE AND TELL PEOPLE ABOUT THE NEW LIFE GOD HAS PROMISED THOSE WHO BELIEVE IN HIS SON, JESUS CHRIST.

THE NEXT MORNING THE HIGH PRIEST CALLS THE JEWISH COURT INTO SESSION AND ORDERS THE DISCIPLES BROUGHT BEFORE IT. WHEN THE OFFICERS RETURN...

THE PRISON IS LOCKED AND THE GUARDS ARE ON DUTY! BUT WHEN WE OPENED THE DOORS THERE WAS NO ONE THERE!

NOT THERE? WHERE ARE THEY?

AT THAT MOMENT A PRIEST ENTERS THE ROOM.

THE MEN YOU PUT IN JAIL LAST NIGHT ARE IN THE TEMPLE TEACHING ABOUT JESUS!

THE HIGH PRIEST ORDERS THE DISCIPLES BROUGHT TO THE COURT AT ONCE.

DIDN'T WE WARN YOU NOT TO PREACH ABOUT JESUS?

WE MUST OBEY GOD RATHER THAN MEN!

AT THIS REPLY THE COURT IS SO ANGRY THAT IT WANTS THE DISCIPLES KILLED AT ONCE. BUT GAMALIEL, A FAMOUS TEACHER, QUICKLY ORDERS THE DISCIPLES TAKEN OUTSIDE. THEN HE TURNS TO THE COURT.

BE CAREFUL OF THE ACTION YOU TAKE AGAINST THESE MEN. IF THIS TEACHING IS THEIR OWN IDEA, IT WILL FAIL. BUT IF IT IS FROM GOD YOU CANNOT DEFEAT THEM -- AND YOU WILL FIND YOURSELVES IN THE AWFUL POSITION OF FIGHTING GOD.

THE COURT IS FORCED TO ADMIT THE WISDOM OF THIS ADVICE. ANGRILY IT ORDERS THE DISCIPLES BEATEN, THEN RELEASES THEM WITH A THREAT OF MORE PUNISHMENT IF THEY CONTINUE PREACHING ABOUT JESUS.

THE DISCIPLES LEAVE...

I'M PROUD TO BE ABLE TO SUFFER FOR JESUS. WE'LL KEEP RIGHT ON WORKING FOR HIM.

ONE OF THEM -- STEPHEN -- IS SOON RECOGNIZED AS A FINE PREACHER.

IN SPITE OF THREATS THE DISCIPLES GO ON PREACHING AND HEALING. THE NUMBER OF FOLLOWERS INCREASES SO MUCH THAT THE TWELVE DISCIPLES DECIDE OTHERS MUST BE CHOSEN TO HELP WITH THE WORK. SEVEN DEACONS ARE SELECTED.

HIS FORMER FRIENDS IN THE SYNAGOGUE CHALLENGE HIM TO A DEBATE ABOUT JESUS. TO THEIR EMBARRASSMENT THEY FIND THEY ARE NO MATCH FOR STEPHEN'S WISDOM AND ABILITY TO DEFEND HIS FAITH. SECRETLY THEY PLOT THEIR REVENGE.

WE MUST BE CAREFUL NOT TO TURN THE PEOPLE AGAINST US.

RIGHT -- BUT IF WE HANDLE IT PROPERLY WE CAN USE THE PEOPLE THEMSELVES TO HELP US DESTROY STEPHEN.

# Martyr for Christ

ACTS 6:11—8:4

STEPHEN PREACHES SUCH POWERFUL SERMONS THAT MANY PEOPLE IN JERUSALEM BECOME FOLLOWERS OF JESUS.

THE JEWISH TEACHERS CHALLENGE HIM TO DEBATES, BUT THEY ARE NO MATCH FOR HIM. THIS MAKES THEM ANGRY, AND THEY PLOT TO GET RID OF HIM.

HERE'S SOME MONEY—SPREAD THE WORD AROUND JERUSALEM THAT STEPHEN IS PREACHING AGAINST THE LAW GOD GAVE TO MOSES.

THAT WILL TURN EVERY GOOD JEW IN JERUSALEM AGAINST STEPHEN.

THE PLOT WORKS -- STEPHEN IS ARRESTED AND BROUGHT BEFORE THE SANHEDRIN, THE SAME COURT THAT CONDEMNED JESUS TO DEATH.

BOLDLY STEPHEN ANSWERS HIS ENEMIES...

YOUR FATHERS PERSECUTED THE PROPHETS WHO TOLD ABOUT THE COMING OF GOD'S CHOSEN ONE -- AND NOW **YOU** HAVE MURDERED **HIM.** YOU ARE THE ONES WHO RECEIVED GOD'S LAW, AND **YOU** ARE THE ONES WHO HAVE DISOBEYED IT!

THE COURT RISES UP IN RAGE, BUT STEPHEN CONTINUES.

I SEE THE HEAVENS OPEN AND JESUS STANDING AT THE RIGHT HAND OF GOD!

AT THIS THE MEMBERS OF THE COURT, LIKE A PACK OF SAVAGE BEASTS, SEIZE STEPHEN AND RUSH HIM OUTSIDE THE CITY. THERE THE PAID WITNESSES THROW THEIR OUTER GARMENTS ON THE GROUND AND ASK A YOUNG MAN NAMED PAUL TO GUARD THEM. AS STEPHEN IS STONED HE PRAYS, "LORD JESUS, RECEIVE MY SPIRIT." THEN WITH HIS LAST BREATH...

LORD, FORGIVE THEM FOR THIS SIN.

THE STONING OF STEPHEN SERVES AS A SIGNAL FOR THE ENEMIES OF JESUS TO ATTACK ALL OF HIS FOLLOWERS. BEFORE THE DAY IS OVER PAUL BEGINS RAIDING HOMES AND DRAGGING MEN AND WOMEN OFF TO PRISON.

NO! MY CHILDREN!

SOON THERE WON'T BE MANY FRIENDS OF JESUS LEFT IN JERUSALEM—THEN THE WHOLE MOVEMENT WILL DIE OUT.

REMEMBERING THE APOSTLES' STRANGE ESCAPE FROM PRISON, THE PERSECUTORS SEEM AFRAID TO ARREST THEM. BUT RAIDS AGAINST THE OTHER DISCIPLES CONTINUE, AND THEY ARE FORCED TO FLEE FOR THEIR LIVES.

WE MUST ESCAPE AT ONCE. I'M NOT A COWARD, BUT MY FAMILY--

JESUS SAID THAT IF WE WERE PERSECUTED IN ONE CITY WE SHOULD FLEE TO ANOTHER.

TWO BIG CARAVANS ARE LEAVING BY THE NORTH GATE TOMORROW MORNING. IF WE'RE CAREFUL WE CAN JOIN THEM AND NOT BE SEEN.

EARLY THE NEXT MORNING TRADERS LEAD THEIR CAMEL TRAINS OUT OF THE CITY, AND IN THEIR MIDST...

WHEREVER WE GO WE'LL TAKE OUR FAITH IN JESUS WITH US.

AND AS WE TEACH OTHERS WE'LL BE HELPING TO SPREAD THE GOSPEL AS JESUS ASKED US TO DO.

AND SO, BY DRIVING JESUS FRIENDS OUT OF JERUSALEM, JEWISH LEADERS, UNKNOWINGLY, CAUSE HIS TEACHINGS TO BE SPREAD THROUGHOUT ALL PALESTINE--EVEN AMONG THEIR ENEMIES, THE SAMARITANS!

# Simon, the Magician

ACTS 8:5-26

TO ESCAPE PERSECUTION AT THE HANDS OF THE JEWISH LEADERS, THOUSANDS OF JESUS' FOLLOWERS FLEE FROM JERUSALEM. PHILIP, ONE OF THE DEACONS OF THE JERUSALEM CHURCH, GOES NORTH TO SAMARIA.

SAMARITANS HATE JEWS. BUT THEY, TOO, ARE LOOKING FOR A SAVIOR, SO I MUST TELL THEM THAT HE HAS COME.

TO PHILIP'S SURPRISE THE SAMARITANS LISTEN EAGERLY AS HE TELLS THEM ABOUT JESUS, AND THEY WATCH WITH WONDER AS HE LOVINGLY HEALS THEIR SICK.

IN THE NAME OF JESUS CHRIST, STAND UP AND WALK!

I CAN STAND--ALONE! TELL ME MORE ABOUT JESUS SO THAT I CAN BECOME HIS FOLLOWER, TOO.

SOON, EVERYONE IN SAMARIA IS TALKING ABOUT PHILIP.

SIMON, THIS MAN PHILIP CAN DO GREATER THINGS THAN YOU CAN. HE CAN HEAL THE SICK, MAKE THE LAME WALK, AND--

HE CAN? WHERE CAN I FIND HIM?

SIMON, THE MOST FAMOUS MAGICIAN IN SAMARIA, HURRIES OFF TO FIND PHILIP.

I THOUGHT I KNEW ALL THE TRICKS OF MAGIC.

WHEN HE FINDS PHILIP HE WATCHES WITH AMAZEMENT THE MIRACLES OF HEALING. BUT HE ALSO LISTENS TO WHAT PHILIP SAYS, AND AFTER A WHILE...

I BELIEVE IN JESUS, TOO. BAPTIZE ME, AND LET ME GO WITH YOU TO LEARN MORE.

WHEN REPORTS OF PHILIP'S WORK REACH THE DISCIPLES IN JERUSALEM, PETER AND JOHN GO TO VISIT SAMARIA. AND AS THEY LAY THEIR HANDS ON THESE NEW FRIENDS OF JESUS, THE HOLY SPIRIT COMES UPON THEM.

THIS IS THE MOST WONDERFUL THING I HAVE EVER SEEN.

SELL ME THIS POWER THAT YOU HAVE.

SIMON! MONEY WILL NOT BUY THIS HOLY GIFT. YOU HAVE NO PLACE IN GOD'S WORK, FOR I CAN SEE THAT YOUR HEART IS FILLED WITH WICKEDNESS. REPENT, AND PRAY THAT GOD WILL FORGIVE YOU.

THE BIBLE DOES NOT SAY WHETHER SIMON TRULY REPENTS. HIS NAME IS NEVER MENTIONED AGAIN.

SOON AFTER THIS PETER AND JOHN RETURN TO JERUSALEM. BUT PHILIP REMAINS, AND ONE NIGHT GOD SENDS HIM NEW INSTRUCTIONS.

PHILIP! ARISE AND GO DOWN THE ROAD THAT RUNS FROM JERUSALEM TO GAZA.

WITHOUT KNOWING THE REASON FOR HIS JOURNEY, OR WHERE IT MAY TAKE HIM, PHILIP OBEYS...

# On the Gaza Road

ACTS 8:26-40; 9:32-35

"GO DOWN TO THE ROAD THAT LEADS TO GAZA," AN ANGEL OF GOD TELLS PHILIP. PHILIP OBEYS, AND AS HE WALKS ALONG THE HOT DESERT HIGHWAY A CHARIOT COMES UP BEHIND HIM. HE LOOKS BACK, AND AT THAT MOMENT THE HOLY SPIRIT SPEAKS UP TO HIM: "GO UP TO THE CHARIOT--AND KEEP CLOSE TO IT."

WHO COULD BE IN THAT CHARIOT THAT GOD HAS SENT ME ALL THIS WAY TO MEET?

AGAIN PHILIP OBEYS. NEARING THE CHARIOT, HE HEARS A MAN READING FROM THE SCRIPTURES.

"HE WAS LED AS A SHEEP TO THE SLAUGHTER."

DO YOU UNDERSTAND WHAT THE PROPHET ISAIAH IS SAYING?

HOW CAN I UNLESS SOMEONE HELPS ME? WILL YOU?

EAGERLY PHILIP GETS INTO THE CHARIOT. THE MAN INTRODUCES HIMSELF AS TREASURER FOR CANDACE, QUEEN OF ETHIOPIA. THEN HE TURNS BACK TO THE SCROLL.

IS THE PROPHET TALKING ABOUT HIMSELF -- OR SOMEONE ELSE?

ABOUT JESUS CHRIST, THE SON OF GOD. HIS ENEMIES CRUCIFIED HIM, BUT GOD RAISED HIM FROM THE DEAD.

AS THEY RIDE ALONG PHILIP EXPLAINS THAT GOD LOVED THE WORLD SO MUCH THAT HE SENT HIS SON JESUS TO DIE FOR OUR SINS, AND WHOEVER TRUSTS IN HIM WILL LIVE FOREVER WITH GOD.

I BELIEVE IN JESUS, AND I'M SORRY FOR EVERYTHING WRONG I HAVE DONE. IS THERE ANY REASON WHY I CANNOT BE BAPTIZED AND BECOME ONE OF HIS FOLLOWERS?

I'M SURE THAT'S WHAT GOD SENT ME HERE TO DO.

SO THE MAN FROM ETHIOPIA IS BAPTIZED... AND THEN HE CONTINUES HIS JOURNEY, EAGER TO TELL THE GOOD NEWS ABOUT JESUS TO HIS OWN PEOPLE.

PHILIP GOES NORTH, PREACHING IN THE TOWNS ALONG THE RIM OF THE MEDITERRANEAN SEA. IN CAESAREA, THE ROMAN CAPITAL IN PALESTINE, HE MAKES HIS HOME.

ABOUT THIS TIME A MIRACULOUS THING HAPPENS--PAUL, WHO HAS BEEN PERSECUTING JESUS' FRIENDS, HAS A WONDERFUL EXPERIENCE. ON THE WAY TO DAMASCUS, JESUS APPEARS TO HIM. PAUL KNOWS THAT JESUS IS THE SAVIOR WHOM GOD RAISED FROM THE DEAD. SO, INSTEAD OF PERSECUTING JESUS' FOLLOWERS, PAUL BECOMES A FOLLOWER, TOO.

WHEN THE DISCIPLES HEAR THIS THEY REJOICE, FOR NOW THEY CAN TRAVEL ALL OVER PALESTINE TEACHING AND HEALING IN THE NAME OF JESUS WITHOUT FEAR OF PAUL ARRESTING THEM.

Sea of Galilee

CAESAREA

JOPPA

LYDDA

JERUSALEM

GAZA

Mediterranean Sea

Dead Sea

WHILE PETER IS PREACHING IN LYDDA...

MY FRIEND, AENEAS, HAS BEEN PARALYZED FOR EIGHT YEARS. CAN YOU HELP HIM?

I CAN'T -- BUT THE SON OF GOD CAN. COME, LET'S GO SEE YOUR FRIEND.

IN THE HOME OF AENEAS PETER LOOKS DOWN ON THE BEDRIDDEN MAN.

JESUS CHRIST HEALS YOU. ARISE.

AENEAS STANDS UP. HE LOOKS IN AWE AT HIS STRONG ARMS AND LEGS.

JESUS MUST LOVE ME VERY MUCH TO RESTORE MY STRENGTH. TELL ME MORE ABOUT HIM SO THAT I CAN BECOME HIS FOLLOWER, TOO.

WHEN THE PEOPLE SEE AENEAS -- WELL AND STRONG -- THEY BELIEVE IN JESUS, TOO. PETER STAYS IN LYDDA, PREACHING, UNTIL ONE DAY TWO MEN FROM THE SEAPORT OF JOPPA ARRIVE IN THE CITY.

WHERE'S PETER? WE MUST FIND HIM AT ONCE!

**158**

# Mission to Joppa

WHILE PETER IS PREACHING IN LYDDA TWO MEN FROM JOPPA COME TO HIM WITH AN URGENT REQUEST: "DORCAS, ONE OF JESUS' FOLLOWERS, JUST DIED. YOU RESTORED AENEAS' HEALTH; CAN YOU HELP DORCAS?" PETER GOES WITH THE MEN AT ONCE, AND WHEN THEY REACH JOPPA...

HER BODY HAS BEEN PLACED IN THE ROOM UPSTAIRS.

THEY FIND DORCAS' HOUSE FILLED WITH WEEPING FRIENDS.

SHE WAS THE KINDEST PERSON I EVER KNEW. SEE THIS COAT--SHE MADE IT FOR ME.

I KNOW HOW MUCH YOU LOVED HER. NOW, IF YOU WILL PLEASE GO OUTSIDE.

ALONE, PETER KNEELS DOWN AND PRAYS. AS HE RISES HE TURNS TO THE BODY OF THE DEAD WOMAN...

DORCAS, GET UP!

INSTANTLY DORCAS OPENS HER EYES. PETER HELPS HER TO RISE, THEN HE PRESENTS HER TO THE PEOPLE WHO HAVE BEEN WAITING OUTSIDE.

GIVE THANKS TO GOD-- YOUR FRIEND IS ALIVE!

AT THE SIGHT OF DORCAS SOME OF THE WOMEN FALL ON THEIR KNEES, WEEPING FOR JOY. OTHERS RUSH OUT INTO THE STREETS TO TELL THE EXCITING NEWS.

DORCAS IS ALIVE!

SHH -- PEOPLE WILL THINK YOU'RE LOSING YOUR MIND. DORCAS IS DEAD -- AND EVERYONE KNOWS IT.

NO! NO! PETER, THE DISCIPLE OF JESUS, BROUGHT HER BACK TO LIFE. COME, SEE FOR YOURSELF!

NOT BELIEVING, BUT CURIOUS, THE WOMAN HURRIES TO DORCAS' HOME.

IT'S TRUE! IT'S TRUE! OH, GOD BE PRAISED!

THE NEWS SPREADS QUICKLY THROUGHOUT JOPPA, AND SOON GREAT CROWDS COME TO PETER, BEGGING TO BE TAUGHT ABOUT JESUS. PETER CONTINUES TO PREACH IN JOPPA UNTIL...

ONE DAY A STRANGE THING HAPPENS IN THE HOME OF CORNELIUS, A ROMAN CENTURION LIVING IN THE SEACOAST CITY OF CAESAREA, SOME THIRTY MILES NORTH. IT IS THREE O'CLOCK IN THE AFTERNOON. CORNELIUS, WHO IN HIS YEARS OF SERVICE IN PALESTINE HAS LEARNED TO WORSHIP GOD, KNEELS TO PRAY.

# God, a Roman, and a Jew

ACTS 10 : 2—11 : 1

ONE AFTERNOON AS CORNELIUS, AN OFFICER OF THE ROMAN ARMY, KNEELS TO PRAY, HE HAS A VISION -- AN ANGEL OF GOD APPEARS AND CALLS HIM BY NAME.

WHAT IS IT?

YOUR PRAYERS AND GOOD WORKS ARE PLEASING TO GOD. SEND MEN TO JOPPA FOR A MAN NAMED PETER. HE IS STAYING WITH SIMON, THE TANNER, WHOSE HOUSE IS BY THE SEA.

WHEN THE ANGEL DISAPPEARS, CORNELIUS SENDS THREE OF HIS MOST TRUSTED MEN AT ONCE TO JOPPA. AS THEY APPROACH THE CITY, THE MAN FOR WHOM THEY ARE SEARCHING GOES TO THE ROOFTOP TO PRAY...

HE, TOO, HAS A VISION. AND A VOICE COMMANDS HIM: "GET UP, PETER; KILL AND EAT."

NEVER, LORD. IN ALL MY LIFE I HAVE NEVER EATEN ANYTHING THAT THE JEWISH LAW CALLS UNCLEAN.

THE VOICE REPLIES: "YOU MUST NOT CALL WHAT GOD HAS CLEANSED UNCLEAN." ALL THIS IS REPEATED THREE TIMES; THEN THE VISION DISAPPEARS. WHILE PETER IS WONDERING WHAT IT MEANS THE HOLY SPIRIT SPEAKS TO HIM: "THREE MEN ARE HERE LOOKING FOR YOU. GO WITH THEM AND HAVE NO DOUBTS, FOR I HAVE SENT THEM TO YOU."

PETER HURRIES DOWNSTAIRS -- AND FINDS THREE MEN AT THE GATE INQUIRING FOR HIM.

I AM THE MAN YOU ARE LOOKING FOR. WHAT DO YOU WANT?

CORNELIUS, A ROMAN CENTURION WHO WORSHIPS GOD, WAS COMMANDED BY AN ANGEL TO SEND FOR YOU.

THE NEXT DAY PETER AND SIX OF HIS FRIENDS SET OUT WITH THE THREE MEN FOR CAESAREA. AS THEY ENTER THE HOME OF CORNELIUS, THE ROMAN CENTURION FALLS ON HIS KNEES TO WORSHIP PETER.

NO--NO-- I AM A MAN LIKE YOURSELF.

163

THEY ENTER THE HOUSE--AND FIND IT FILLED WITH ROMANS.

ACCORDING TO JEWISH LAW, GENTILES -- YOU PEOPLE OF ANOTHER NATION -- ARE UNCLEAN. THEREFORE, AS A JEW, I AM FORBIDDEN TO ASSOCIATE WITH YOU. BUT GOD HAS TOLD ME IN A VISION THAT NO MAN MUST BE CALLED UNCLEAN. SO I HAVE COME AS YOU ASKED. WHAT DO YOU WANT OF ME?

AN ANGEL OF GOD TOLD ME TO SEND FOR YOU. AND WE ARE WAITING TO LEARN WHAT THE LORD HAS COMMANDED YOU TO TELL US.

I SEE NOW THAT ANY MAN, JEW OR GENTILE, WHO LOVES GOD AND DOES WHAT IS RIGHT, IS ACCEPTABLE TO HIM.

THEN PETER TELLS THEM THAT JESUS WAS THE SAVIOR SENT FROM GOD TO GIVE ETERNAL LIFE TO ALL WHO BELIEVE IN HIM. WHEN PETER SEES THAT THE HOLY SPIRIT HAS COME TO THE GENTILES, HE HAS HIS CHRISTIAN FRIENDS BAPTIZE THEM.

SUCH NEWS TRAVELS FAST, AND WHEN IT REACHES THE CHURCH IN JERUSALEM...

HOW DARE PETER BREAK JEWISH LAWS AND ASSOCIATE WITH GENTILES?

# Angel—Open Gate

ACTS 11:1—12:14

THE NEWS THAT PETER HAS BEEN ASSOCIATING WITH GENTILES REACHES JERUSALEM BEFORE HE DOES--AND SEVERAL OF THE CHURCH MEMBERS ARE WAITING TO QUESTION HIM.

> IS IT TRUE THAT YOU ARE BREAKING OUR JEWISH LAWS AND BEING FRIENDLY TOWARD GENTILES--EVEN EATING WITH THEM AND VISITING IN THEIR HOMES?

> GOD DIRECTED A ROMAN CENTURION TO SEND FOR ME, AND GOD TOLD ME TO GO TO HIM. I OBEYED, AND WHILE I WAS TELLING THE GENTILES ABOUT JESUS, THE HOLY SPIRIT CAME TO THEM -- THE SAME AS TO US ON THE DAY OF PENTECOST. IF GOD GAVE THEM THE SAME GIFT THAT HE GAVE TO US, WHO WAS I TO STAND IN THE WAY?

THE MEMBERS AGREE WITH PETER -- AND PRAISE GOD FOR GIVING ETERNAL LIFE TO THE GENTILES. THE CHURCH CONTINUES TO GROW...

SO JAMES, ONE OF THE FOUR FISHERMEN WHO LEFT THEIR NETS TO FOLLOW JESUS, IS SLAIN TO SATISFY A WICKED KING'S STRUGGLE FOR POWER.

BUT ON THE NIGHT BEFORE HEROD PLANS TO SENTENCE PETER, AN ANGEL OF GOD ENTERS THE PRISON CELL...

GET UP! PUT ON YOUR SANDALS, WRAP YOUR CLOAK AROUND YOU, AND FOLLOW ME.

AS PETER OBEYS THE CHAINS FALL FROM HIS WRISTS -- AND THE ANGEL LEADS HIM OUT OF THE PRISON CELL.

WHEN THEY APPROACH THE GREAT IRON GATE IN THE PRISON WALL, IT OPENS! THEY GO OUT INTO THE CITY STREETS, AND -- SUDDENLY -- THE ANGEL VANISHES!

SCARCELY BELIEVING WHAT HAS HAPPENED, PETER HURRIES TO THE HOME OF MARY, THE MOTHER OF HIS YOUNG FRIEND, MARK. THERE HE POUNDS ON THE DOOR OF THE GATE UNTIL RHODA, A SERVANT GIRL, ANSWERS.

IT'S PETER!

BUT INSTEAD OF LETTING HIM IN, RHODA TURNS AND RUNS BACK INTO THE HOUSE...

# Fall of a Tyrant

ACTS 12: 14-24

IT IS NIGHT IN JERUSALEM. PETER HAS JUST BEEN RESCUED FROM PRISON BY AN ANGEL AND IS SEEKING ADMITTANCE AT THE HOME OF A FRIEND. WHEN THE SERVANT GIRL RECOGNIZES HIS VOICE, SHE RUSHES BACK INTO THE HOUSE.

IT'S PETER!

PETER? O RHODA, YOU'RE SO UPSET THAT YOU'RE IMAGINING THINGS.

THE GIRL INSISTS. FINALLY SOME OF THE GROUP, WHO HAVE GATHERED TO PRAY FOR PETER, ACCOMPANY HER TO THE GATE.

IF YOU KNEW IT WAS PETER, WHY DIDN'T YOU LET HIM IN?

I WAS SO EXCITED-- I HAD TO TELL YOU.

168

CAUTIOUSLY THEY OPEN THE DOOR...

PETER! IT **IS** YOU! COME IN--QUICKLY!

DID HEROD RELEASE YOU?

NO-- BUT GOD DID. AN ANGEL AWAKENED ME AND TOLD ME TO FOLLOW. I DID-- AND THE PRISON GATES OPENED BEFORE US. IN THE STREET, THE ANGEL DISAPPEARED. TELL THE OTHERS THAT I AM FREE. AND NOW I MUST GET OUT OF JERUSALEM BEFORE HEROD LEARNS WHAT HAS HAPPENED.

THE FRIENDS OF PETER REJOICE AND THANK GOD FOR HIS ESCAPE, BUT THE NEXT MORNING WHEN HEROD DISCOVERS THAT HIS PRISONER IS GONE--

YOU SAY HE WAS CHAINED TO TWO GUARDS, AND OTHERS WERE GUARDING THE DOOR, YET YOU EXPECT ME TO BELIEVE THAT HE JUST DISAPPEARED? WHAT WERE THE GUARDS DOING? SEARCH THE CITY. FIND PETER OR THOSE TRAITORS WILL PAY FOR THIS WITH THEIR LIVES!

BUT THE SEARCH FAILS.

A FEW DAYS LATER HEROD APPEARS AT A PUBLIC CELEBRATION IN CAESAREA. THERE, DRESSED IN A DAZZLING ROBE OF SILVER, HE GOES OUT AND SPEAKS TO THE PEOPLE. TO FLATTER HIM, THEY SHOUT:

IT IS THE VOICE OF A GOD--NOT A MAN!

HEROD ACCEPTS THE PRAISE WHICH SHOULD HAVE BEEN GIVEN ONLY TO GOD. SUDDENLY GOD STRIKES HIM DOWN, AND A FEW DAYS LATER HE DIES.

WITH THE DEATH OF HEROD, THE PERSECUTION OF THE CHURCH STOPS FOR A TIME. THE GOOD NEWS OF JESUS CHRIST CONTINUES TO SPREAD THROUGHOUT THE LAND OF THE JEWS...

# The Story of Paul

ACTS 7:58—8:4; 9:1-3a; 22:3

## Adventurer for Christ

BOLDLY HE FACES ANGRY MOBS... CROSSES MOUNTAINS... AND SAILS THE STORMY SEAS TO PREACH THE GOOD NEWS THAT JESUS IS THE SON OF GOD AND SAVIOR OF THE WORLD.

THE EXCITING STORY OF THIS GREAT MISSIONARY BEGINS LONG AGO...

A FEW YEARS AFTER THE BIRTH OF JESUS PAUL* IS BORN IN TARSUS. THE SON OF GOOD JEWISH PARENTS, HE IS BROUGHT UP TO WORSHIP AND OBEY GOD.

WHAT WILL YOU DO WHEN YOU GROW UP, PAUL?

I DON'T KNOW YET, BUT WHATEVER I DO, IT WILL BE FOR GOD, AND IT WILL BE EXCITING.

*HIS JEWISH NAME IS SAUL.

HE TAKES THE FIRST STEP TOWARD MAKING HIS DREAM COME TRUE WHEN HE GOES TO JERUSALEM TO STUDY. THERE HE MEETS SOME OF THE SAME TEACHERS THAT JESUS TALKED WITH ONLY A FEW YEARS BEFORE.

IN TIME PAUL BECOMES THE MOST BRILLIANT PUPIL OF THE FAMOUS TEACHER, GAMALIEL. TOGETHER THEY DISCUSS THE SCRIPTURES-- ESPECIALLY THE PARTS THAT TELL ABOUT THE COMING OF THE SAVIOR.

LIKE KING DAVID, HE WILL MAKE OUR COUNTRY STRONG AND POWERFUL. IF ONLY HE WOULD COME NOW -- I'D SPEND MY LIFE SERVING HIM.

BUT LIKE MOST JEWISH LEADERS, PAUL REFUSES TO ACCEPT JESUS AS THE SAVIOR FOR WHOM THE JEWS ARE WAITING. WHEN THEY STONE STEPHEN, ONE OF JESUS' FOLLOWERS, PAUL STANDS BY -- WATCHING.

ANY MAN WHO FOLLOWS JESUS DESERVES TO DIE!

PAUL SOON BEGINS HIS OWN ATTACK ON JESUS' FOLLOWERS. HE RAIDS THEIR HOMES AND DRAGS THEM OFF TO BE QUESTIONED, PUNISHED, EVEN PUT TO DEATH.

NO! NO! MY CHILDREN!

THE FOLLOWERS OF JESUS FLEE FOR THEIR LIVES. WHEN PAUL LEARNS THAT THEY ARE SPREADING THEIR TEACHING WHEREVER THEY GO, HE IS EVEN MORE FURIOUS.

THEY MUST BE STOPPED BEFORE THEY STIR UP PEOPLE EVERYWHERE. ALREADY THEY ARE AS FAR NORTH AS DAMASCUS.

WHAT CAN WE DO?

WITH SOME STRONG-ARMED MEN, PAUL SETS OUT ON A 190-MILE JOURNEY TO DAMASCUS. HIS EXCITEMENT MOUNTS WITH EVERY MILE, FOR HE BELIEVES WITH ALL HIS HEART THAT IN DESTROYING JESUS' FOLLOWERS HE IS SERVING GOD...

# A Light and a Voice

ACTS 9:3-22

PAUL RIDES TOWARD DAMASCUS WITH THE EAGERNESS OF A HUNTER ON THE TRACK OF HIS PREY. AT THE SIGHT OF THE CITY IN THE DISTANCE, HE URGES HIS HORSE ON -- AS IF EVERY MINUTE COUNTED IN HIS SEARCH TO DESTROY JESUS' FOLLOWERS.

SUDDENLY HE IS SURROUNDED BY A LIGHT BRIGHTER THAN THE NOONDAY SUN. HE FALLS TO THE GROUND -- AND A VOICE CALLS HIM BY HIS JEWISH NAME: "SAUL! SAUL, WHY ARE YOU PERSECUTING ME?"

WHO ARE YOU?

I AM JESUS OF NAZARETH, WHOM YOU ARE PERSECUTING.

WHAT DO YOU WANT ME TO DO?

"GO INTO THE CITY," JESUS ANSWERS, "AND YOU WILL BE TOLD WHAT TO DO."

175

THE MEN WITH PAUL ARE TERRIFIED BY WHAT HAS HAPPENED.

PAUL, WHAT'S THE MATTER?

MY EYES—I CAN'T SEE! HELP ME INTO THE CITY.

SO, BLIND, AND AWED BY HIS EXPERIENCE, THE ONCE-PROUD PAUL IS LED INTO DAMASCUS-- DOWN A STREET CALLED STRAIGHT.

WHERE ARE YOU TAKING ME?

TO THE HOME OF JUDAS, A FRIEND OF MINE.

IN DARKNESS PAUL PRAYS AND WAITS. ON THE THIRD DAY HE CALLS TO HIS HOST.

HAS A MAN NAMED ANANIAS ASKED TO SEE ME?

NO. WHAT MAKES YOU EXPECT HIM?

I HAVE BEEN PRAYING, AND IN A VISION I HAVE SEEN A MAN BY THAT NAME COMING TO RESTORE MY SIGHT.

IF HE COMES I'LL BRING HIM TO YOU AT ONCE.

# Man with a Mission

ACTS 9:27-30; 11:22-25

PAUL RETURNS TO JERUSALEM ONLY TO FIND THAT JESUS' FRIENDS BELIEVE HE IS STILL THEIR ENEMY. AT THE SIGHT OF HIM THEY HIDE. BUT BARNABAS, THE MAN WHO SOLD HIS FARM AND GAVE THE MONEY FOR THE POOR, IS NOT AFRAID. HE LISTENS TO PAUL-- AND TAKES HIM TO PETER.

PAUL SAYS HE IS NOW A FOLLOWER OF JESUS--AND I BELIEVE HIM.

BRING HIM IN.

FOR DAYS AND NIGHTS PAUL, THE BRILLIANT STUDENT OF JEWISH LAW, AND PETER, THE RUGGED FISHERMAN FROM GALILEE, TALK ABOUT THEIR LORD AND SAVIOR.

JESUS' LAST COMMAND DIRECTED US TO GO INTO ALL THE WORLD AND PREACH THE GOSPEL.

I'M GLAD HE TRUSTS ME TO HELP CARRY OUT THAT COMMAND.

179

BUT JESUS' FOLLOWERS AGAIN LEARN OF THE PLOT AGAINST PAUL'S LIFE, AND WARN HIM.

YOUR ENEMIES ARE POWERFUL MEN, PAUL, AND THEY WILL NOT STOP UNTIL THEY HAVE PUT AN END TO YOUR WORK IN JERUSALEM. LET US HELP YOU ESCAPE.

YOU ARE RIGHT! I CAN SERVE MY LORD ELSEWHERE.

WITH THE HELP OF FRIENDS, PAUL ESCAPES TO THE SEACOAST. THEN HE SAILS NORTH TO HIS BOYHOOD HOME OF TARSUS. THERE HE EARNS HIS LIVING BY MAKING TENTS -- AND DEVOTES THE REST OF HIS TIME TO TELLING PEOPLE THAT JESUS IS THE PROMISED SAVIOR.

ONE DAY A SHIP DOCKS AT TARSUS... A PASSENGER HURRIES DOWN THE PLANK.

NOW TO FIND PAUL!

# Foreign Assignment

ACTS 11:25-30; 12:25—13:7

AFTER ESCAPING FROM HIS ENEMIES IN JERUSALEM, PAUL RETURNS TO HIS BOYHOOD HOME OF TARSUS. FOR SEVERAL YEARS HE WORKS AND PREACHES THE GOSPEL. ONE DAY AN OLD FRIEND COMES TO SEE HIM...

BARNABAS! WHAT BRINGS YOU TO TARSUS?

YOU, PAUL! I HAVE BEEN PREACHING IN ANTIOCH, AND THE CHURCH HAS GROWN SO MUCH THAT I NEED HELP. WILL YOU COME?

EAGERLY PAUL ACCEPTS THE INVITATION.

THE CHURCH WAS STARTED BY PEOPLE WHO FLED FROM YOUR PERSECUTION IN JERUSALEM.

THANK GOD YOU ARE GIVING ME THE CHANCE TO ASK THEIR FORGIVENESS AND WORK WITH THEM IN SPREADING THE GOSPEL.

IN ANTIOCH, THE THIRD LARGEST CITY OF THE ROMAN EMPIRE,
PAUL AND BARNABAS WIN BOTH JEWS AND GENTILES TO FAITH IN CHRIST.
HERE THE FOLLOWERS OF JESUS ARE GIVEN THE NAME OF CHRISTIANS!

AFTER A TIME TEACHERS FROM JERUSALEM COME TO VISIT THE GROWING CHURCH. ONE OF THEM, AGABUS, MAKES A TRAGIC PROPHECY.

I HAVE RECEIVED A WARNING FROM GOD THAT A GREAT FAMINE IS COMING. MANY OF OUR PEOPLE IN JERUSALEM ARE POOR. THEY WILL STARVE UNLESS--

PAUL INTERRUPTS EXCITEDLY.

LET US ALL GIVE WHAT MONEY WE CAN. I'LL HELP DELIVER IT!

BUT YOU HAVE ENEMIES IN JERUSALEM!

AND OUR LORD HAS FOLLOWERS THERE! WE MUST HELP THEM IN SPITE OF THE DANGER.

182

THE ANTIOCH CHRISTIANS GIVE GENEROUSLY, AND PAUL AND BARNABAS SET OUT FOR JERUSALEM WHERE THE FEAR OF HUNGER IS IN EVERY HOME.

WHAT WILL WE DO WHEN OUR FOOD IS GONE?

GOD WILL NOT FORSAKE US.

LISTEN-- SOMEONE'S AT THE DOOR.

BARNABAS!

PAUL AND I BRING HELP FROM THE CHRISTIANS IN ANTIOCH.

TAKE WORD TO THE OTHER ELDERS. WE MUST PURCHASE FOOD AND TAKE IT TO OTHERS AT ONCE.

TO THINK I EVER DOUBTED!

THEIR MISSION OVER, PAUL AND BARNABAS PREPARE TO LEAVE JERUSALEM.

PAUL, THIS IS MY COUSIN, MARK. HE WOULD LIKE TO GO WITH US.

GOOD! WE CAN USE YOU, MARK.

IN ANTIOCH THEY MEET WITH OTHERS FOR PRAYER. GOD TELLS THE LEADERS OF THE CHURCH THAT HE WANTS PAUL AND BARNABAS TO TAKE THE GOOD NEWS OF JESUS TO OTHER LANDS. THE TWO MEN ACCEPT THE CALL -- AND SET OUT WITH MARK.

THERE'S CYPRUS -- THE ISLAND WHERE I WAS BORN!

AND THAT'S WHERE OUR MISSIONARY WORK BEGINS.

AFTER PREACHING IN SEVERAL CITIES OF THE ISLAND, THE MISSIONARIES REACH THE CAPITAL, PAPHOS.

HOW EAGER THE PEOPLE ARE TO HEAR ABOUT JESUS.

YES, AND SO FAR THERE'S NO TROUBLE FROM ANYONE.

BY ORDER OF SERGIUS PAULUS, THE ROMAN GOVERNOR, COME WITH ME!

AFTER A TOUR ACROSS THE ISLAND OF CYPRUS, PAUL, BARNABAS, AND YOUNG MARK REACH THE CAPITAL. TO THEIR SURPRISE, THE ROMAN GOVERNOR CALLS THEM BEFORE HIM AND ASKS TO HEAR ABOUT JESUS. EAGERLY PAUL TELLS ABOUT JESUS AND HOW GOD RAISED HIM FROM THE DEAD. AT THIS THE COURT MAGICIAN RISES UP IN ANGER...

LIES! ALL LIES! NO MAN CAN DIE AND LIVE AGAIN!

YOU CHILD OF THE DEVIL! IT IS TIME YOU STOPPED TRYING TO TURN PEOPLE FROM THE RIGHT WAYS OF THE LORD. NOW HIS HAND IS UPON YOU -- AND FOR A TIME YOU WILL BE BLIND!

186

188

THIS MAN IS A LIAR—AND A TRAITOR TO THE FAITH OF OUR FATHERS.
WE FELT IT OUR DUTY TO GIVE GOD'S MESSAGE OF EVERLASTING LIFE TO YOU JEWS FIRST, BUT IF YOU DO NOT WANT THE MESSAGE, WE'LL TAKE IT TO THE GENTILES!

THE GENTILES REACT WITH JOY AND THANKSGIVING.
THANK GOD FOR SENDING PAUL WITH SUCH GOOD NEWS!
ETERNAL LIFE WITH GOD—I MUST TELL MY FRIENDS AT ONCE!

BUT THE JEWS ARE SO ANGRY THAT THEY CARRY THEIR CAMPAIGN OF LIES AGAINST PAUL TO THE LEADING CITIZENS OF ANTIOCH.
DON'T YOU SEE? PAUL IS TRYING TO CAUSE TROUBLE BETWEEN JEWS AND GENTILES. IF IT LEADS TO BLOODSHED THE GOVERNMENT IN ROME WILL SEND SOLDIERS TO INVESTIGATE--
WE KNOW HOW TO HANDLE TROUBLEMAKERS! PAUL AND HIS FRIEND MUST LEAVE AT ONCE --OR BE PUNISHED!

# Miracle in Lystra

ACTS 13:51—14:19

TO ESCAPE PERSECUTION, PAUL AND BARNABAS ARE FORCED TO LEAVE ANTIOCH. THEY GO SOUTHEAST ABOUT 80 MILES TO ICONIUM, ANOTHER CITY IN THE PROVINCE OF GALATIA. THERE JEWS AND GREEKS ALIKE ACCEPT THE GOOD NEWS OF JESUS. THIS ANGERS THE JEWISH LEADERS --

PAUL! BARNABAS! YOU MUST LEAVE AT ONCE! THERE'S A PLOT UNDER WAY TO STONE YOU!

DON'T WORRY -- YOU HAVE FRIENDS HERE WHO WILL FIGHT TO PROTECT YOU.

WE CANNOT LET YOU RISK YOUR LIVES FOR US. WE MUST LEAVE -- BUT KEEP STRONG IN YOUR FAITH, AND HELP THE OTHERS.

THE MISSIONARIES ESCAPE AND HURRY ON TO THE CITY OF LYSTRA. ONE DAY AS PAUL IS PREACHING, HE NOTICES A LAME MAN LISTENING WITH KEEN INTEREST.

STAND UP ON YOUR FEET!

INSTANTLY THE MAN JUMPS UP.

I CAN WALK. GLORY TO GOD, I CAN WALK!

THESE STRANGERS ARE NOT ORDINARY MEN THEY ARE GODS WHO LOOK LIKE MEN!

THE PEOPLE SPEAK IN THE LANGUAGE OF LYSTRA, SO PAUL AND BARNABAS DO NOT UNDERSTAND HOW THE CROWD FEELS UNTIL THEY SEE A PRIEST BRINGING ANIMALS FOR SACRIFICE.

NO! NO! YOU MUST NOT WORSHIP US. WE ARE MEN, JUST LIKE YOU, BUT WITH A MESSAGE FROM THE ONE TRUE GOD. HE IS THE ONE WHO HEALED THE MAN!

190

BUT YOU ARE LIKE THE GODS JUPITER AND MERCURY.

JUPITER AND MERCURY ARE FALSE GODS. WORSHIP THE TRUE GOD WHO HAS SENT YOU RAIN FROM HEAVEN AND FRUIT IN ITS SEASON.

THE PEOPLE LISTEN EAGERLY. BUT, UNKNOWN TO PAUL AND BARNABAS, THEIR ENEMIES FROM ANTIOCH AND ICONIUM FOLLOW THEM TO LYSTRA. THEY SPREAD THEIR LIES AMONG THE SIMPLE PEOPLE.

PAUL AND BARNABAS CAUSE TROUBLE WHEREVER THEY GO. GET RID OF THEM AS WE DID!

THERE'LL BE NO TROUBLE IN LYSTRA. I'LL SEE TO THAT!

SO A MOB IS WHIPPED INTO ACTION!

THERE'S PAUL! STONE HIM!

# Storm Warning
ACTS 14:19—15:1

WHIPPED INTO A RAGE BY MEN FROM ANTIOCH AND ICONIUM, THE PEOPLE OF LYSTRA TURN AGAINST PAUL AND STONE HIM.

WHEN THE STONING IS FINISHED, THE ANGRY MOB DRAGS PAUL'S BODY OUT OF THE CITY.

QUICKLY BARNABAS AND CHRISTIANS OF LYSTRA GATHER AROUND PAUL'S MOTIONLESS FORM. BUT AS THEY STAND WEEPING...

HE'S GETTING UP! THANK GOD, HE LIVES! HE LIVES!

PAUL! WE THOUGHT THEY HAD KILLED YOU!

THEY MEANT TO, BUT GOD HAS SAVED MY LIFE FOR A PURPOSE. COME, LET'S GO BACK INTO THE CITY.

BACK TO LYSTRA? THAT MOB WILL NEVER LET YOU OUT ALIVE!

GOD WILL PROTECT ME.

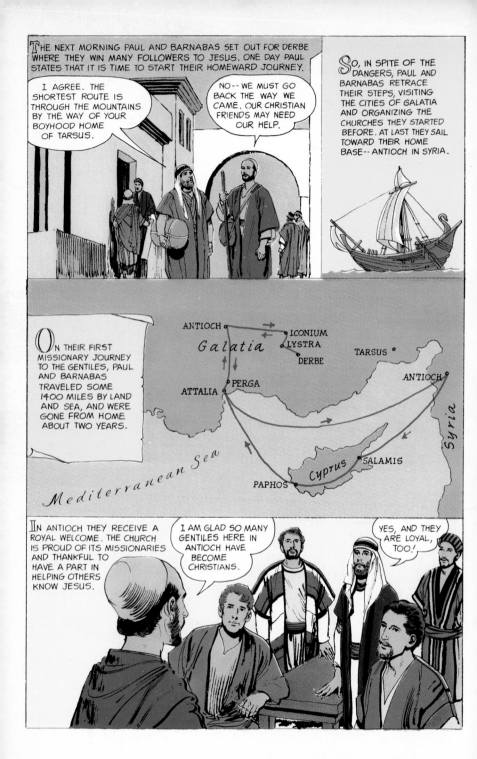

THE NEXT MORNING PAUL AND BARNABAS SET OUT FOR DERBE WHERE THEY WIN MANY FOLLOWERS TO JESUS. ONE DAY PAUL STATES THAT IT IS TIME TO START THEIR HOMEWARD JOURNEY.

I AGREE. THE SHORTEST ROUTE IS THROUGH THE MOUNTAINS BY THE WAY OF YOUR BOYHOOD HOME OF TARSUS.

NO-- WE MUST GO BACK THE WAY WE CAME. OUR CHRISTIAN FRIENDS MAY NEED OUR HELP.

SO, IN SPITE OF THE DANGERS, PAUL AND BARNABAS RETRACE THEIR STEPS, VISITING THE CITIES OF GALATIA AND ORGANIZING THE CHURCHES THEY STARTED BEFORE. AT LAST THEY SAIL TOWARD THEIR HOME BASE-- ANTIOCH IN SYRIA.

ON THEIR FIRST MISSIONARY JOURNEY TO THE GENTILES, PAUL AND BARNABAS TRAVELED SOME 1400 MILES BY LAND AND SEA, AND WERE GONE FROM HOME ABOUT TWO YEARS.

ANTIOCH
ICONIUM
LYSTRA
Galatia
DERBE
TARSUS
ANTIOCH
PERGA
ATTALIA
Syria
SALAMIS
Cyprus
PAPHOS
Mediterranean Sea

IN ANTIOCH THEY RECEIVE A ROYAL WELCOME. THE CHURCH IS PROUD OF ITS MISSIONARIES AND THANKFUL TO HAVE A PART IN HELPING OTHERS KNOW JESUS.

I AM GLAD SO MANY GENTILES HERE IN ANTIOCH HAVE BECOME CHRISTIANS.

YES, AND THEY ARE LOYAL, TOO!

194

WITH PAUL AND BARNABAS AS LEADERS, THE CHURCH IN ANTIOCH GROWS IN SIZE AND INFLUENCE. BUT ONE DAY A GROUP OF JEWISH CHRISTIANS FROM THE CHURCH IN JERUSALEM ARRIVES.

YOU GENTILES CANNOT BECOME CHRISTIANS UNLESS YOU FIRST PROMISE TO OBEY OUR JEWISH LAWS!

BY WHAT AUTHORITY DO YOU SAY THAT?

BY THE AUTHORITY OF JAMES, THE BROTHER OF JESUS, WHO IS NOW LEADER IN THE CHURCH IN JERUSALEM.

HOW CAN THIS BE TRUE? PAUL DOES NOT SAY SO. WHAT SHALL WE DO?

I DON'T KNOW. I'LL NEVER GIVE UP MY FAITH IN JESUS, BUT I CAN'T OBEY ALL THOSE JEWISH LAWS.

THEN YOU CANNOT BE A CHRISTIAN!

THE QUARREL GROWS -- JEWISH CHRISTIANS VERSUS GENTILE CHRISTIANS. THE CHURCH IN ANTIOCH IS IN DANGER OF SPLITTING IN TWO!

# Council in Jerusalem

ACTS 15:1-13; GALATIANS

Like A VIOLENT WIND, A DISAGREEMENT BETWEEN THE JEWISH AND GENTILE CHRISTIANS RIPS THROUGH THE ANTIOCH CHURCH, DIVIDING THE MEMBERS. UNKNOWN TO PAUL AND BARNABAS, WHO ARE STRUGGLING TO KEEP THE CHURCH UNITED, ANOTHER STORM IS BUILDING UP IN THE AREA OF THEIR FIRST MISSIONARY JOURNEY...

I HATE TO TELL PAUL OUR PROBLEM.

YES, BUT THE CHURCHES ARE IN TROUBLE-- AND SO IS HE!

INSIDE THE CITY THE MEN FIND PAUL AND GIVE HIM THEIR MESSAGE.

THE CHURCHES YOU STARTED IN GALATIA ARE IN TROUBLE. SOME JEWISH CHRISTIANS CLAIM THAT GOD SENT JESUS TO BE **THEIR** SAVIOR, AND IF WE GENTILES WANT TO BECOME CHRISTIANS WE MUST FIRST BECOME JEWS.

THEY ALSO QUESTION YOUR RIGHT TO PREACH THE GOSPEL BECAUSE YOU WERE NOT ONE OF JESUS' DISCIPLES. YOUR KNOWLEDGE, THEY SAY, IS SECONDHAND.

THE SAME PROBLEM HAS DIVIDED OUR CHURCH HERE. BUT THE ISSUE IS BIGGER THAN THE CHURCHES IN GALATIA AND ANTIOCH. THE WHOLE CHURCH OF CHRIST IS THREATENED.

THEN YOU CAN'T GO BACK WITH US?

NOT NOW. THE ELDERS HERE HAVE ASKED BARNABAS AND ME TO GO TO JERUSALEM TO TALK THIS PROBLEM OVER WITH JESUS' DISCIPLES. BUT I'LL WRITE A LETTER WHICH YOU CAN TAKE BACK WITH YOU.

# Second Journey

ACTS 15:13—16:8

THE JERUSALEM COUNCIL FACES A PROBLEM THAT IS DIVIDING THE CHURCH: MUST GENTILES BECOME JEWS AND OBEY ALL THEIR RULES BEFORE THEY CAN BECOME CHRISTIANS? THE ARGUMENTS ARE PRESENTED. THE COUNCIL TURNS TO JAMES, BROTHER OF JESUS AND HEAD OF THE COUNCIL.

BROTHERS, LET US NOT MAKE IT HARD FOR GENTILES TO BECOME CHRISTIANS. WE SHOULD ASK ONLY THAT THEY OBEY A FEW NECESSARY RULES. THEY MUST AVOID EATING FOOD THAT HAS BEEN OFFERED TO IDOLS, AND THEY MUST LEAD PURE LIVES.

THE COUNCIL AGREES, AND TWO OF ITS MEMBERS, JUDAS BARSABAS AND SILAS, JOIN PAUL AND BARNABAS IN TAKING THE DECISION TO ANTIOCH.

198

THE NEWS IS RECEIVED WITH JOY IN ANTIOCH THAT JEWS AND GENTILES CAN GO ON WORKING TOGETHER FOR JESUS. WITH THIS SETTLED, PAUL IS FREE TO CONTINUE HIS MISSIONARY WORK IN GENTILE COUNTRIES.

BARNABAS, LET'S MAKE A TRIP TO VISIT THE CHURCHES WE STARTED.

GOOD IDEA-- I'D LIKE TO ASK MARK TO GO WITH US AGAIN.

NO -- MARK LEFT US BEFORE.

I KNOW, BUT WE SHOULD GIVE HIM ANOTHER CHANCE.

PAUL DISAGREES, SO BARNABAS TAKES MARK AND SAILS TO THE ISLAND OF CYPRUS. PAUL TAKES SILAS WITH HIM BY LAND TO VISIT THE CHURCHES HE STARTED.

IN LYSTRA, THE CITY IN WHICH HE HAD BEEN STONED, PAUL FINDS A GROWING CHURCH.

PAUL, I WANT YOU TO MEET TIMOTHY. HE'S BECOME ONE OF OUR BEST YOUNG LEADERS.

I'VE HEARD MANY FINE REPORTS OF YOU, TIMOTHY. WOULD YOU LIKE TO GO WITH SILAS AND ME?

THERE GOOD FORTUNE AWAITS THE TRAVELERS.

TIMOTHY EAGERLY ACCEPTS, AND THE CHURCH GIVES ITS BLESSING. SOON THE THREE TRAVELERS ARE ON THEIR WAY. GOD TELLS THEM NOT TO FOLLOW THE TRADE ROUTE TO EPHESUS, SO THEY GO NORTH AND WEST UNTIL THEY REACH TROAS ON THE AEGEAN SEA

DR. LUKE! THE LORD MUST HAVE LED YOU TO JOIN US HERE.

PAUL! I WILL TRAVEL WITH YOU.

AS THE FOUR MISSIONARIES WALK THROUGH THE STREETS OF THE GREAT SEAPORT...

ONE HUNDRED AND FIFTY MILES ACROSS THE SEA LIES MACEDONIA, THE LAND FROM WHICH ALEXANDER THE GREAT BEGAN HIS CONQUEST OF THE WORLD.

I WONDER WHERE GOD WANTS ME TO PREACH NEXT...

200

# Call from Across the Sea

ACTS 16:9-19

PAUL AND HIS COMPANIONS, SILAS, TIMOTHY, AND DR. LUKE ARE DIRECTED BY THE HOLY SPIRIT TO TROAS. THERE THEY AWAIT FURTHER ORDERS. ONE NIGHT PAUL HAS A VISION.

COME OVER TO MACEDONIA AND HELP US!

EARLY THE NEXT MORNING...

GOD HAS CALLED US TO TAKE THE GOOD NEWS OF JESUS TO MACEDONIA!

WONDERFUL! I'LL ARRANGE PASSAGE ON THE FIRST BOAT SAILING NORTHWEST.

A GOOD WIND SPEEDS THE FOUR MISSIONARIES ACROSS THE AEGEAN SEA TO THE PORT OF NEAPOLIS. FROM THERE THEY WALK EIGHT MILES TO THE CITY OF PHILIPPI.

THE CITY HAS NO SYNAGOGUE, SO ON THE SABBATH THEY WORSHIP BY A RIVERSIDE.

DO YOU HEAR THOSE WOMEN? THEY ARE PRAYING TO GOD.

THE MISSIONARIES JOIN THE WORSHIPERS -- AND SOON PAUL IS TELLING THEM ABOUT JESUS. A LADY CLOTH MERCHANT, NAMED LYDIA, SPEAKS FIRST.

GOD HAS OPENED MY HEART TO BELIEVE IN HIS SON, JESUS. MAY I BE BAPTIZED?

OF COURSE, LYDIA.

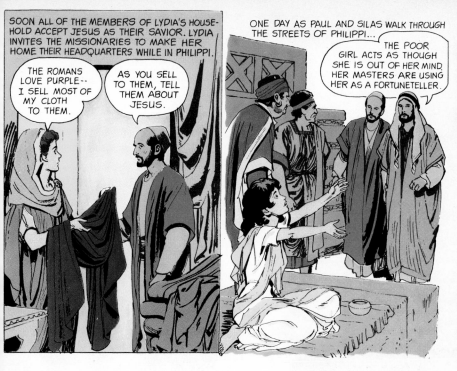

SOON ALL OF THE MEMBERS OF LYDIA'S HOUSEHOLD ACCEPT JESUS AS THEIR SAVIOR. LYDIA INVITES THE MISSIONARIES TO MAKE HER HOME THEIR HEADQUARTERS WHILE IN PHILIPPI.

THE ROMANS LOVE PURPLE-- I SELL MOST OF MY CLOTH TO THEM.

AS YOU SELL TO THEM, TELL THEM ABOUT JESUS.

ONE DAY AS PAUL AND SILAS WALK THROUGH THE STREETS OF PHILIPPI...

THE POOR GIRL ACTS AS THOUGH SHE IS OUT OF HER MIND. HER MASTERS ARE USING HER AS A FORTUNETELLER.

IN THE NAME OF JESUS, YOU ARE CURED.

YOU ARE A MAN OF GOD!

LOOK! SHE CAN'T TELL FORTUNES ANY MORE. OUR BUSINESS IS RUINED. WHAT'LL WE DO?

WHOEVER THAT MAN IS, HE'LL PAY FOR MEDDLING IN OUR AFFAIRS. COME ON!

# Earthquake

PAUL RESTORES TO HER RIGHT MIND A GIRL WHO WAS A FORTUNETELLER FOR SOME GREEDY MEN. ANGRY BECAUSE THEIR BUSINESS HAS BEEN RUINED, THE MEN DRAG PAUL AND SILAS BEFORE THE JUDGES IN THE PUBLIC SQUARE. A CROWD GATHERS.

THESE MEN ARE JEWS. THEY ARE TRYING TO MAKE TROUBLE BY TEACHING THINGS AGAINST ROMAN LAW.

YES! WE ALL HEARD HIM!

BUT I--

SILENCE! THERE'LL BE NO TROUBLE IN THIS CITY. GIVE THESE MEN A BEATING AND THROW THEM IN JAIL. AND SEE THAT THEY DON'T ESCAPE.

[AF]TER A SEVERE BEATING, PAUL AND SILAS ARE TAKEN [TO] PRISON AND PUT IN STOCKS.

YOU'LL PAY WITH YOUR LIFE IF THESE MEN ESCAPE.

[IN] SPITE OF THEIR SUFFERING, THE [CH]RISTIAN MISSIONARIES PRAY AND [SI]NG THEIR PRAISES TO GOD.

SUDDENLY—AT MIDNIGHT—THE PRISON FOUNDATION TREMBLES. THE WALLS TWIST AND CRACK-- SNAPPING CHAINS AND HINGES FROM THE HEAVY DOORS.

EARTHQUAKE!

205

WHEN THE QUAKE IS OVER THE JAILER RUSHES DOWN INTO THE DUNGEON, AFRAID THAT HIS PRISONERS HAVE ESCAPED.

THEY'RE GONE! I MIGHT AS WELL KILL MYSELF.

NO! NO! WE'RE ALL HERE!

BELIEVING THAT PAUL AND SILAS HAD SOMETHING TO DO WITH THE EARTHQUAKE THE JAILER FALLS ON HIS KNEES BEFORE THEM.

WHAT MUST I DO TO BE SAVED?

BELIEVE ON THE LORD JESUS CHRIST.

THE JAILER QUICKLY TAKES THE TWO PRISONERS TO HIS HOUSE AND TREATS THEIR WOUNDED BODIES. HE AND HIS FAMILY LISTEN EAGERLY AS PAUL TELLS THEM ABOUT JESUS -- AND ALL ARE BAPTIZED.

EARLY IN THE MORNING ROMAN OFFICERS COME TO THE PRISON.

THE JUDGES HAVE ORDERED YOUR RELEASE.

WE ARE ROMAN CITIZENS, YET WE HAD NO TRIAL. NOW THE JUDGES THINK THEY CAN GET RID OF US QUIETLY. TELL THE JUDGES THEMSELVES TO COME AND MAKE OUR RELEASE AS PUBLIC AS OUR BEATING.

# Out of Trouble . . . Into Trouble

THE ROMAN JUDGES, WHO ORDERED PAUL AND SILAS RELEASED FROM PRISON, ARE SURPRISED WHEN THE OFFICER RETURNS WITH A MESSAGE FROM THE PRISONERS.

THOSE MEN ARE ROMAN CITIZENS. THEY DEMAND THAT YOU COME TO THE PRISON AND RELEASE THEM AS PUBLICLY AS YOU PUNISHED THEM.

ROMAN CITIZENS? AND WE SENTENCED THEM WITHOUT A TRIAL! THIS COULD MEAN TROUBLE FOR US.

FORGETTING THEIR DIGNITY THE JUDGES GO IMMEDIATELY TO THE PRISON.

WE ARE TRULY SORRY FOR THE WAY WE TREATED YOU. NOW PLEASE LEAVE THE CITY TO AVOID FURTHER TROUBLE.

WE FORGIVE YOU-- AND WE WILL LEAVE TODAY.

AT THE HOUSE OF LYDIA, PAUL, SILAS, AND TIMOTHY BID THEIR FRIENDS GOOD-BYE.

THANK YOU FOR LEAVING DR. LUKE HERE TO LEAD OUR CHURCH.

WE WILL RETURN SOMEDAY. HOLD FAST TO YOUR FAITH IN JESUS AND HELP OTHERS TO KNOW HIM.

TRAVELING ON SOME 90 MILES, THE MISSIONARIES REACH THESSALONICA ON THE AEGEAN SEA. PAUL GOES AT ONCE TO THE SYNAGOGUE TO PREACH.

THE SCRIPTURES PROMISED THAT A SAVIOR WOULD COME. JESUS, WHO DIED ON THE CROSS AND ROSE FROM THE DEAD, IS THAT SAVIOR.

MANY PEOPLE LISTEN AND BELIEVE -- BUT SOME OF THE JEWISH LEADERS DO NOT.

WE'VE GOT TO GET RID OF HIM BEFORE HE HAS THE WHOLE CITY BELIEVING WHAT HE SAYS.

HE'S STAYING AT JASON'S HOUSE. LET'S GET HIM THERE.

GATHERING A STRONG-ARMED MOB, THE JEWISH LEADERS CALL ON JASON.

IF YOU'RE LOOKING FOR PAUL, HE'S NOT HERE.

YOU'RE HIDING HIM. IF YOU WON'T LET US HAVE HIM, WE'LL TAKE YOU.

# Paul Explains the "Unknown God"

ACTS 17:13—18:12; I AND II THESSALONIANS

TO ESCAPE THEIR ENEMIES IN THESSALONICA, PAUL AND HIS COMPANIONS, SILAS AND TIMOTHY, GO ON TO BEREA. BUT UNKNOWN TO PAUL, HIS ENEMIES FOLLOW HIM.

WE'VE COME TO WARN YOU ABOUT A JEW NAMED PAUL. HE'S A TROUBLEMAKER! DRIVE HIM OUT OF THE CITY AS WE DID.

WE'LL GET RID OF HIM RIGHT NOW!

BUT BEFORE THE ANGRY MOB CAN FIND PAUL, HIS FRIENDS HELP HIM ESCAPE TO ATHENS. FROM THERE PAUL SENDS WORD FOR SILAS AND TIMOTHY TO FOLLOW AS SOON AS POSSIBLE.

IN THE GREAT GREEK CITY--

IDOLS! IDOLS EVERYWHERE! EVEN AN ALTAR TO AN "UNKNOWN GOD."

ON THE SABBATH PAUL PREACHES TO THE JEWS, BUT DURING THE WEEK HE CARRIES HIS MESSAGE OF JESUS TO THE GREEKS IN THE MARKET PLACE.

HE SAYS THERE IS ONLY ONE GOD, AND THAT HE SENT HIS ONLY SON, JESUS, TO HELP US.

I'D LIKE TO HEAR MORE ABOUT A GOD WHO CARES FOR PEOPLE. LET'S ASK THIS MAN TO SPEAK BEFORE THE COURT OF MARS' HILL.

PAUL ACCEPTS THE INVITATION EAGERLY.

GENTLEMEN OF ATHENS, SINCE YOU WORSHIP A GOD YOU DO NOT KNOW, I'LL TELL YOU WHO HE IS -- THE TRUE GOD, WHO MADE ALL THINGS. HE DOES NOT LIVE IN TEMPLES MADE BY HUMAN HANDS. HE IS NOT FAR FROM EACH ONE OF US, FOR IN HIM WE LIVE, AND MOVE, AND HAVE OUR BEING.

THE MEN OF ATHENS LISTEN EAGERLY -- UNTIL PAUL SAYS THAT JESUS ROSE FROM THE DEAD.

NOBODY CAN BE RAISED FROM THE DEAD. WHAT A SILLY IDEA!

I'M NOT SO SURE...

211

IT IS DOING WELL, BUT THE PEOPLE ARE HAVING A HARD TIME.

I'LL WRITE TO THEM AT ONCE.

## PAUL'S First Letter to the Thessalonians, WHICH IS A BOOK OF THE NEW TESTAMENT.

To the church of the Thessalonians-- from Paul, Silas, and Timothy

We remember how joyfully you turned from idols to serve the true God. Though we had to leave, it was good to receive news that you are standing true to your faith, even though people have been making it hard for you.

As we urged you when we were with you, live in the way that will please God, who invited you to have a place in His Kingdom. Keep on praying, and love one another more and more. I know you have worried about Christians who have died, but you need not. For Jesus promised that when He comes back from Heaven these will meet Him.

Be sure this letter is read to all the members of the church.

PAUL GETS FURTHER WORD FROM HIS FRIENDS IN THESSALONICA. HE WRITES A

## Second Letter to the Thessalonians.
THIS ALSO IS A BOOK OF THE NEW TESTAMENT.

To the church of the Thessalonians-- from Paul, Silas, and Timothy

Don't get a mistaken idea of what I told you. No one should quit working because he thinks Jesus will return right away. If anyone will not work, he should not be fed. Before Jesus comes, there will be a time when an evil man tries to rule the world, taking the place of God. But God will keep you from evil. Don't get discouraged in doing what is right.

In any letter that I send to you, I write a few words at the close in my own handwriting--like this--so that you will be sure the letter is from me. May Christ's love be with you all.

FOR A YEAR AND A HALF PAUL PREACHES IN CORINTH. A STRONG CHRISTIAN CHURCH IS STARTED. BUT THE JEWISH LEADERS ARE ANGRY AT PAUL AND LOOK UPON HIM AS A TRAITOR TO HIS RELIGION.

GALLIO IS A NEW GOVERNOR. HE WON'T RISK HAVING TROUBLE BREAK OUT RIGHT AWAY. I THINK WE CAN WORK THINGS SO THAT **HE** WILL GET RID OF PAUL FOR US!

# Talk of the Town

ACTS 18:13—19:16

JEWISH LEADERS IN CORINTH ARE ANGRY BECAUSE PAUL IS WINNING SO MANY PEOPLE TO JESUS. THEY TAKE HIM BEFORE THE NEW ROMAN GOVERNOR.

MOST EXCELLENT GALLIO-- THIS MAN IS TELLING PEOPLE TO WORSHIP GOD IN WAYS THAT ARE AGAINST THE LAW. HE IS CHANGING THE JEWISH CUSTOMS WHICH THE ROMANS PERMIT.

PAUL IS ABOUT TO DEFEND HIMSELF, BUT TO EVERYONE'S SURPRISE GALLIO TURNS ON PAUL'S ENEMIES.

I WILL TAKE NO PART IN QUARRELS ABOUT THE JEWISH RELIGION. THIS HAS NOTHING TO DO WITH ROMAN LAW. NOW, GET OUT OF COURT!

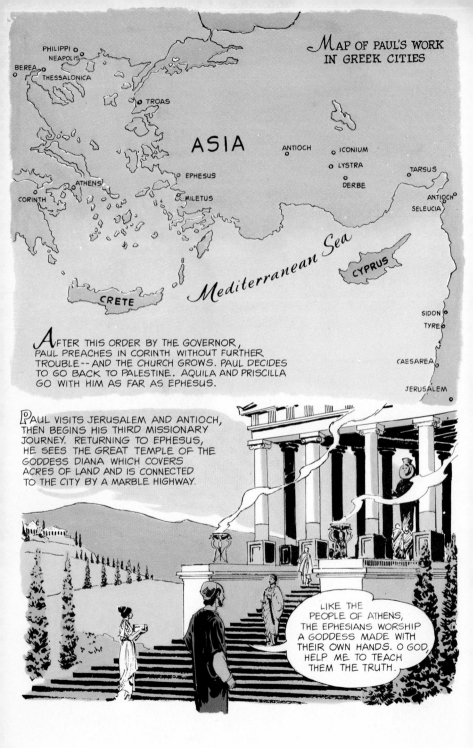

MAP OF PAUL'S WORK IN GREEK CITIES

ASIA

PHILIPPI
NEAPOLIS
BEREA
THESSALONICA
TROAS
ATHENS
CORINTH
EPHESUS
MILETUS
ANTIOCH
ICONIUM
LYSTRA
DERBE
TARSUS
ANTIOCH
SELEUCIA

Mediterranean Sea

CRETE

CYPRUS

SIDON
TYRE
CAESAREA
JERUSALEM

AFTER THIS ORDER BY THE GOVERNOR, PAUL PREACHES IN CORINTH WITHOUT FURTHER TROUBLE -- AND THE CHURCH GROWS. PAUL DECIDES TO GO BACK TO PALESTINE. AQUILA AND PRISCILLA GO WITH HIM AS FAR AS EPHESUS.

PAUL VISITS JERUSALEM AND ANTIOCH, THEN BEGINS HIS THIRD MISSIONARY JOURNEY. RETURNING TO EPHESUS, HE SEES THE GREAT TEMPLE OF THE GODDESS DIANA WHICH COVERS ACRES OF LAND AND IS CONNECTED TO THE CITY BY A MARBLE HIGHWAY.

LIKE THE PEOPLE OF ATHENS, THE EPHESIANS WORSHIP A GODDESS MADE WITH THEIR OWN HANDS. O GOD, HELP ME TO TEACH THEM THE TRUTH.

# The Angry Mob

**ACTS 19:17—20; I CORINTHIANS**

T HE PEOPLE OF EPHESUS SEE THAT WHAT PAUL SAYS IS TRUE AND THAT THE MAGICIANS ARE FAKES. MANY PERSONS BELIEVE IN CHRIST AND BURN THEIR BOOKS OF MAGIC.

PAUL IS STILL REJOICING WITH THE GROWTH OF THE CHURCH IN EPHESUS WHEN NEWS COMES FROM CORINTH...

PAUL DICTATES A LETTER TO THE CHURCH OF CORINTH, KNOWN AS *I Corinthians,* IT IS A BOOK OF THE NEW TESTAMENT.

THE CHURCH IN CORINTH IS HAVING ALL SORTS OF TROUBLES. THE MEMBERS ARE TAKING SIDES AGAINST ONE ANOTHER. SOME OF THEM SAY YOU ARE THE HEAD OF OUR CHURCH. OTHERS SAY APOLLOS IS THE BEST PREACHER -- AND STILL OTHERS SAY PETER IS THE REAL LEADER CHOSEN BY JESUS.

*Paul, to the church at Corinth...*

I beg of you, my brothers, do not quarrel and divide the church. There is only one head of the Christian Church -- Christ! It was Christ -- not Paul or Apollos or Peter -- who died for you on the cross.

Keep yourselves pure. Don't you see that you yourselves are the temple of God -- and that God's Spirit lives in you? God will destroy anyone who defiles his temple, for his temple is holy -- and that is what you are!

If I knew everything and could speak like an angel but did not have Christian love, I would amount to nothing. Be kind and love one another in the church. I send my love to all of you.

THE CHURCH IN EPHESUS GROWS — ALMOST AS RAPIDLY AS THE BLAZE WHICH DESTROYED THE BOOKS OF MAGIC. IT HAS ITS EFFECT ON THE IDOL MERCHANTS OF THE CITY...

BUSINESS IS NO GOOD. PEOPLE AREN'T BUYING SILVER TEMPLES OF DIANA.

IT'S BECAUSE OF THAT CHRISTIAN PREACHER, PAUL. HE IS LEADING THE PEOPLE TO BELIEVE IN JESUS.

217

THE CROWD GROWS AS IT PUSHES THROUGH THE STREETS -- SOON THE WHOLE CITY IS IN AN UPROAR...

GREAT IS DIANA OF THE EPHESIANS!

AND THE MOB TAKES PAUL'S FRIENDS TO THE GREAT OUTDOOR THEATER.

A FEW MINUTES LATER IN ANOTHER PART OF THE CITY...

PAUL! THE SILVERSMITHS ARE AFTER YOU FOR DESTROYING THEIR BUSINESS. THEY HAVE SEIZED GAIUS AND ARISTARCHUS AND...

WHERE ARE THEY?

NO! PAUL! THAT MOB WILL KILL YOU!

# Riot in Ephesus

**ACTS 19:31—20:3; II CORINTHIANS AND ROMANS**

CITY OFFICIALS BEG PAUL TO STAY AWAY FROM THE MOB. FOR TWO HOURS THE RIOTERS SHOUT, "GREAT IS DIANA OF THE EPHESIANS." FINALLY THE TOWN CLERK MAKES HIMSELF HEARD...

GENTLEMEN OF EPHESUS -- IF THE SILVERSMITHS HAVE A COMPLAINT, LET THEM BRING IT BEFORE THE COURTS. I WARN YOU -- IF THE ROMAN GOVERNMENT ASKS THE REASON FOR THIS RIOTING, THERE IS NO EXCUSE WE CAN GIVE FOR IT.

IN FACE OF THIS THREAT, THE RIOT BREAKS UP. PAUL SENDS FOR HIS FRIENDS.

THE MOB WAS REALLY AFTER ME -- SO TO PREVENT TROUBLE FOR ALL OF YOU, I WILL GO TO PHILIPPI.

OUR PRAYERS WILL GO WITH YOU.

SOON AFTER PAUL REACHES PHILIPPI, TITUS JOINS HIM WITH NEWS FROM CORINTH.

PAUL, YOUR LETTER TO THE CHRISTIANS AT CORINTH MADE THEM CORRECT THEIR WRONG-DOING. BUT NOW SOME PEOPLE HAVE COME TO CORINTH WHO CLAIM YOU ARE NOT A TRUE APOSTLE OF JESUS.

ONCE AGAIN PAUL WRITES TO THE CHURCH IN CORINTH. THE LETTER--KNOWN AS II *Corinthians*--IS A BOOK OF THE NEW TESTAMENT.

I can see that my letter upset you, but I am glad I sent it. Not because I want to hurt you, but to make you sorry as God would have you sorry for the things that were wrong.

We are taking a collection for poor Christians in Jerusalem. Other churches have given large sums. I trust you will be able to do the same. Let everyone give what he has decided in his own heart to give, for God loves a cheerful giver.

And now, for those who question whether or not I am a true minister of Christ. I have been imprisoned, I have been beaten many times, I have often faced death. I have been stoned, I have been shipwrecked three times--all to carry out the work of Christ. When I visit you again, I hope it will be a happy meeting. Good-bye till then.

WHILE TITUS TAKES THE LETTER TO CORINTH, PAUL CONTINUES VISITING CHURCHES IN MACEDONIA, COLLECTING MONEY FOR THE POOR IN JERUSALEM. MONTHS LATER HE REACHES CORINTH WHERE HE IS GREETED BY FRIENDS WHO HAVE GIVEN EAGERLY TO HIS COLLECTION.

THIS MONEY WILL SHOW THE CHRISTIANS IN JERUSALEM THAT YOU'RE CONCERNED FOR THEM.

# Bound—Hand and Foot

ACTS 20:3—21:14

THE JEWISH BOAST FAILS. WARNED OF THE PLOT, PAUL MAKES A QUICK CHANGE OF PLANS AND TAKES THE LAND ROUTE NORTH TO MACEDONIA.

PAUL OUTWITTED HIS ENEMIES THIS TIME, BUT HOW LONG CAN HE ESCAPE THEIR HATE?

AFTER WEEKS OF TRAVEL AND VISITING CHURCHES ALONG THE WAY, PAUL REACHES TROAS. HE HAS SO MUCH TO TELL THE PEOPLE THAT HE TALKS FAR INTO THE NIGHT. OVERCOME BY SLEEP, A YOUNG MAN FALLS FROM AN UPPER WINDOW...

LOOK OUT!

HE FELL FROM THE THIRD STORY. HE MUST BE DEAD.

DON'T BE ALARMED. HE IS ALIVE.

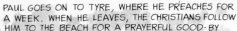

PAUL GOES ON TO TYRE, WHERE HE PREACHES FOR A WEEK. WHEN HE LEAVES, THE CHRISTIANS FOLLOW HIM TO THE BEACH FOR A PRAYERFUL GOOD-BY

DON'T GO TO JERUSALEM. JEWS ARE THERE WAITING TO KILL YOU BECAUSE YOU SAY JESUS IS THE SON OF GOD.

I MUST GO. I HAVE MONEY WHICH GENTILE CHRISTIANS HAVE GIVEN ME FOR THE POOR IN JERUSALEM. I AM NOT AFRAID...

FARTHER DOWN THE COAST AT CAESAREA, PAUL VISITS WITH PHILIP THE EVANGELIST. THE PROPHET AGABUS JOINS THEM, AND--SUDDENLY-- WHILE THEY ARE TALKING HE TAKES PAUL'S BELT AND BEGINS TO BIND HIS OWN HANDS AND FEET.

WHAT DOES THIS MEAN?

THE HOLY SPIRIT TELLS ME THAT THE MAN TO WHOM THE BELT BELONGS WILL BE BOUND-- LIKE THIS-- BY THE JEWS IN JERUSALEM AND HANDED OVER TO THE GENTILES.

PAUL-- GIVE UP YOUR PLANS TO GO TO JERUSALEM. FOR OUR SAKE--

WHY DO YOU TRY TO WEAKEN ME WITH YOUR TEARS? I AM PREPARED NOT ONLY TO BE BOUND, BUT TO DIE FOR THE SAKE OF THE LORD JESUS.

# A Boy and a Secret

ACTS 21:15—23:24

THE DAY AFTER PAUL REACHES JERUSALEM, HE MEETS WITH JAMES AND OTHER LEADERS OF THE JERUSALEM CHURCH. HE DELIVERS THE MONEY FOR THE POOR AND TELLS WHAT GOD HAS DONE IN OTHER LANDS.

I MUST WARN YOU, PAUL, YOU HAVE ENEMIES HERE WHO THINK YOU ARE A TRAITOR. EVEN THE CHRISTIAN JEWS HAVE QUESTIONS BECAUSE OF YOUR WORK AMONG THE GENTILES.

I'LL WORSHIP WITH THEM IN THE TEMPLE TO SHOW THAT I AM TRUE TO THE FAITH OF OUR FATHERS.

JAMES' WARNING COMES TRUE WITHIN THE WEEK. WHILE PAUL IS WORSHIPING IN THE TEMPLE HIS ENEMIES ACCUSE HIM, FALSELY, OF BRINGING GENTILES INTO GOD'S HOUSE WHERE ONLY JEWS ARE ALLOWED.

THERE HE IS -- THE TRAITOR!

HE HAS DEFILED THIS HOLY PLACE OF GOD!

225

IN ANGER THE PEOPLE TURN AGAINST PAUL. A MOB DRAGS HIM FROM THE TEMPLE AND STARTS TO BEAT HIM.

LOOK OUT-- ROMAN SOLDIERS ARE COMING!

NOW, TELL US WHAT THIS MAN HAS DONE.

TAKE HIM AWAY-- KILL HIM!

THE SOLDIERS CARRY PAUL TO THE PRISON. ON ITS STEPS PAUL STOPS AND TELLS THE PEOPLE HOW HE BECAME A CHRISTIAN, BUT WHEN HE MENTIONS PREACHING TO THE GENTILES, THE MOB GOES WILD.

HE IS NOT FIT TO LIVE!

KILL HIM!

KILL HIM!

# Paul Pleads His Case

ACTS 23:25—28:4

To PROTECT PAUL'S LIFE, THE ROMAN COMMANDER AT JERUSALEM SENDS HIM TO CAESAREA, WHERE PAUL IS KEPT IN PRISON. AFTER TWO YEARS PAUL APPEARS BEFORE FESTUS, THE ROMAN GOVERNOR, AND DEMANDS HIS RIGHT TO BE TRIED BY THE EMPEROR NERO AT ROME. BUT FIRST FESTUS BRINGS PAUL BEFORE A NEIGHBORING RULER, KING AGRIPPA, WHO IS VISITING THE CITY.

I ONCE THOUGHT IT MY DUTY TO OPPOSE JESUS. I HAD MANY OF HIS FOLLOWERS IMPRISONED. BUT ON MY WAY TO DAMASCUS I SAW A LIGHT FROM HEAVEN... AND JESUS SAID TO ME, "I SEND YOU TO TURN PEOPLE OF ALL NATIONS FROM THE POWER OF SATAN TO GOD... O KING AGRIPPA, I COULD NOT DISOBEY THE HEAVENLY VISION.

YOU'RE TRYING TO PERSUADE ME TO BE A CHRISTIAN.

Festus and Agrippa would have set Paul free if he had not demanded a trial in Rome. So--under Roman guard and accompanied by Luke-- Paul is taken aboard a ship bound for Rome. At the island of Crete.

THE WINTER STORMS WILL SOON BE HERE. IT WILL BE DANGEROUS TO GO ON UNTIL SPRING.

THE HARBOR AT PHOENIX IS NOT FAR AWAY--WE'LL SPEND THE WINTER THERE.

THE SHIP SETS SAIL--ONLY TO BE STRUCK BY A RAGING "NORTHEASTER."

TAKE DOWN THE MAINSAIL!

ON THE 14TH NIGHT OF THE STORM THE SAILORS TRY TO DESERT THE SHIP.

UNLESS THOSE MEN STAY WITH THE SHIP, YOU CANNOT BE SAVED!

228

THE SOLDIERS CUT THE SMALL BOAT LOOSE --AND THE SAILORS ARE FORCED TO STAY WITH THE SHIP. AT DAYBREAK...

LAND AHEAD!

HEADING TOWARD A BAY, THE SHIP RUNS AGROUND. THE BOW STICKS FAST, BUT THE STERN BEGINS TO BREAK UNDER THE POUNDING OF THE HEAVY WAVES.

ABANDON SHIP!

KILL THE PRISONERS -- IF THEY REACH SHORE THEY'LL ESCAPE.

BECAUSE OF HIS FRIENDSHIP FOR PAUL, THE ROMAN OFFICER SPARES THE PRISONERS. SOLDIERS, SAILORS, PASSENGERS, AND PRISONERS STRUGGLE FOR THEIR LIVES IN THE RAGING SEA.

IN ANSWER TO PAUL'S PRAYERS, ALL 276 MEN ON BOARD REACH LAND SAFELY. PEOPLE ON THE ISLAND OF MALTA RUSH DOWN TO THE SHORE TO HELP THE VICTIMS OF THE WRECK.

I'LL GET SOME MORE WOOD.

WE'LL HAVE A FIRE GOING SOON.

AS PAUL LAYS SOME STICKS ON THE FIRE A SNAKE CRAWLS OUT OF THE BUNDLE-- AND STRIKES!

A VIPER!

THE MAN ACTS AS IF HE DOESN'T KNOW THAT A VIPER'S BITE MEANS AGONY AND DEATH!

HE MUST BE A MURDERER! HE ESCAPED THE SEA --BUT JUSTICE WILL NOT LET HIM LIVE.

230

# Apostle on the March

For months Paul waits--chained to a Roman guard--for his trial before the emperor in Rome. His Christian friends in all the churches pray for him constantly, and one day...

GREETINGS, PAUL, I HAVE COME WITH A GIFT FROM THE CHURCH AT PHILIPPI.

EPAPHRODITUS! WHAT A BLESSING TO HAVE SUCH FRIENDS!

HE TRAVELED OVER 800 MILES JUST TO DELIVER A GIFT!

Soon after reaching Rome Epaphroditus becomes very ill. Christians in the city gladly take care of him...

THANK GOD, YOU ARE RECOVERING. THIS LETTER IS FROM YOUR FRIENDS IN PHILIPPI--THEY ARE WORRIED ABOUT YOU.

I AM SORRY TO HAVE MADE THEM WORRY.

As soon as he is well, Epaphroditus goes to see Paul.

**THE CHURCH IN ROME IS GROWING RAPIDLY. UNLESS YOU NEED ME HERE, I WOULD LIKE TO GO BACK HOME.**

**YES, THAT'S WHAT YOU SHOULD DO. I HAVE WRITTEN A LETTER TO MY FRIENDS IN PHILIPPI. YOU CAN TAKE IT BACK WITH YOU.**

Paul's letter to the *Philippians* is a book of the New Testament.

*To the church at Philippi,*
*I don't know yet how my trial will come out, but I believe God will let me visit you again. Make me happy by living in harmony among yourselves. Think as Christ did. Though divine, He was willing to humble Himself and become a Man—willing even to die on the cross.*
*Thank you for your gift which Epaphroditus brought. You have been generous. God will also supply all that you need. Always be glad, since you are Christians, and think about the things that are good. The Christians here send greetings, especially the ones who are working in Caesar's palace.*

Two years -- and finally Paul's case is brought to court.* Before Nero, the most powerful ruler in the world, Paul makes his defense, and in a few days...

**THANK GOD! NOW I CAN CARRY OUT MY DREAM TO TAKE THE GOSPEL OF CHRIST TO THE FARTHEST CORNERS OF THE EMPIRE!**

**PAUL! PAUL! THE COURT HAS SET YOU FREE!**

*ALTHOUGH THE BIBLE DOES NOT TELL ABOUT PAUL'S RELEASE, THE LETTERS HE WROTE AFTERWARD SHOW THAT IT MUST HAVE TAKEN PLACE.

# The Burning of Rome

## II TIMOTHY

IT IS THE YEAR 64. NERO, THE CRUEL EMPEROR OF ROME, HAS MANY ENEMIES AMONG HIS OWN PEOPLE. THERE ARE RUMORS OF PLOTS AGAINST HIS LIFE. THEN, STRANGELY, A FIRE SWEEPS ACROSS THE CITY. FOR NINE DAYS IT RAGES -- BURNING GREAT SECTIONS OF THE CITY AND DRIVING THOUSANDS FROM THEIR HOMES. FROM HIS PALACE, NERO WATCHES...

EVEN WHILE THE CITY IS STILL IN FLAMES NEW RUMORS SPREAD.

NERO! THE PEOPLE ARE SAYING **YOU** STARTED THE FIRE. THERE ARE UGLY THREATS--

AND I SAY THE CHRISTIANS STARTED THE FIRE. ARREST THEM--TORTURE THEM--KILL THEM!

THIS WILL TURN PEOPLE'S ATTENTION AWAY FROM ME.

ARMED WITH ORDERS FROM THE EMPEROR, SOLDIERS KILL HUNDREDS OF CHRISTIANS IN ROME. THE ORDER REACHES OUT ACROSS THE SEA FROM ITALY-- AND ONCE AGAIN PAUL IS ARRESTED!

BY ORDER OF THE EMPEROR, YOU ARE UNDER ARREST!

ONCE AGAIN PAUL COMES TO ROME--A PRISONER THIS TIME. HE IS CHAINED TO THE WALL OF THE MAMERTINE PRISON. LUKE COMES TO COMFORT HIM.

I'M SURE I HAVE ONLY A FEW MONTHS TO LIVE. BRING SOME PAPER AND **A** PEN AND WRITE WHAT I TELL YOU TO TIMOTHY.

I'LL BRING THE MATERIAL ON MY NEXT VISIT.

WHEN LUKE RETURNS, PAUL TELLS HIM WHAT TO WRITE. THE LETTER, **II Timothy**, IS A BOOK OF THE NEW TESTAMENT.

WHEN TIMOTHY RECEIVES THE LETTER, HE SAILS AT ONCE TO ROME. THERE HE FINDS LUKE, WHO TAKES HIM TO THE PRISON. BUT AS TIMOTHY GREETS PAUL...

I HAVE JUST RECEIVED ORDERS -- YOU ARE UNDER ARREST!

*Dear Timothy,*

*Be strong, like a good soldier for Christ. Remember the truth as you learned from me and from the Holy Scriptures. Keep preaching it, even though the time will come when people don't want to hear the truth.*

*I want to see you very much. Do your best to come before winter. Bring the coat I left at Troas, and the books. I have almost reached the end of my life. Soon I will be with the Lord and He will give me a place in His heavenly Kingdom. Try to come soon.*

*Paul*

SO TIMOTHY, TOO, IS ARRESTED FOR TEACHING ABOUT JESUS. IN THEIR PRISON CELLS THE TWO MISSIONARIES WAIT FOR ROMAN LAW TO BRING THEM TO TRIAL. IN TIME PAUL'S CASE IS CALLED. ALONE, HE IS MARCHED TO THE COURT OF NERO.

# Soldier Victorious

**II TIMOTHY 4: 6-8**

In Rome, Paul is on trial for his life before the cruel emperor, Nero.

I FIND YOU GUILTY OF STIRRING UP TROUBLE IN THE EMPIRE. THE SENTENCE IS DEATH-- BY THE SWORD.

QUICKLY SOLDIERS TAKE PAUL OUTSIDE THE CITY--TO BEHEAD HIM.

I HAVE FOUGHT THE GOOD FIGHT. I HAVE FINISHED MY COURSE. I HAVE KEPT THE FAITH.

SO DEATH COMES TO PAUL, WHO FOUNDED CHRISTIAN CHURCHES ON TWO CONTINENTS AND WHO WAS LED BY GOD TO WRITE NEARLY HALF OF THE BOOKS OF THE NEW TESTAMENT.

BUT PAUL'S DEATH DOES NOT BRING A HALT TO THE GOSPEL. CHRIST'S CHURCH MARCHES ON--THROUGHOUT THE ROMAN EMPIRE, AND THEN ACROSS THE WORLD.

# THE END OF AN ERA

## HEBREWS THROUGH REVELATION

JESUS' DISCIPLES WHO WERE STILL ALIVE WERE GROWING OLD IN THE LATTER HALF OF THE FIRST CENTURY AFTER HIS BIRTH. THEY COULD NOT TRAVEL TO ALL THE CHURCHES, SO THEY TURNED TO WRITING LETTERS TO JESUS' FOLLOWERS.

THE LAST NINE BOOKS OF THE NEW TESTAMENT, HEBREWS THROUGH REVELATION, ARE MESSAGES THESE MEN WROTE TO GIVE ADVICE, COURAGE, AND COMFORT TO THE EARLY CHRISTIANS.

## The Book of Hebrews

THE LETTER TO THE HEBREWS WAS WRITTEN AT A TIME WHEN JEWISH CHRISTIANS WERE BEING PRESSURED BY THE ROMANS AND JEWS TO GIVE UP THEIR FAITH IN JESUS.

THEY ASKED THEMSELVES: WHICH IS RIGHT, FAITH IN JESUS OR FAITH IN THE RELIGION OF OUR FOREFATHERS ABRAHAM, MOSES, AND DAVID?

"GOD HAS SPOKEN TO US THROUGH HIS SON, JESUS," THE LETTER SAID. "ABRAHAM, MOSES, AND DAVID WERE GREAT MEN WHO LIVED BY FAITH. THEY DIED; BUT JESUS CHRIST WILL LIVE FOREVER. HOLD FAST TO YOUR FAITH IN HIM."

THE LETTER ALSO BROUGHT THE GOOD NEWS THAT TIMOTHY HAD BEEN RELEASED FROM PRISON.

## The Book of James

AS LEADER OF THE CHURCH IN JERUSALEM, JAMES, THE BROTHER OF JESUS, WROTE A LETTER OF ADVICE TO CHRISTIANS LIVING IN OTHER COUNTRIES.

*True religion is shown by what you do. Help those who need help. Be fair to all people. Ask God for wisdom, and keep your lives pure.*

THUS THE BROTHER OF JESUS, WHO WAS KNOWN AS JAMES THE JUST, CONTINUED TO SPREAD THE GOSPEL.

## The Book of I Peter

PETER WAS NOW AN OLD MAN. HE COULD SEE THAT THE ROMANS WERE TURNING AGAINST THE CHRISTIANS AND THAT JESUS' FOLLOWERS WOULD BE IN GREAT DANGER. HE HAD SILAS WRITE A LETTER FOR HIM.

*"Face your hardships bravely," Peter told the people. "There is one thing no one can take from you -- the hope of living in Heaven with Christ. Trust in Him; He will reward those who follow Him faithfully."*

## The Book of II Peter

PETER KNEW THAT HE DID NOT HAVE MANY YEARS TO LIVE. HE WANTED TO HELP THE FOLLOWERS OF JESUS TO BE TRUE TO HIM, SO HE SENT THEM THIS LETTER.

"You believe in Jesus," he wrote, "Then act the way His followers should." Then he warned the Christians not to be upset by people who laughed at them because they believed that Jesus would return.
"When the time is right," Peter wrote, "Christ will return.
"God is giving people a chance to repent. He has promised a new world for those who love and obey Him.
"See how important it is for you to live for God!"

THESE ARE THE LAST WORDS WE HEAR FROM THE FISHERMAN WHO GAVE UP HIS NETS TO FOLLOW JESUS.

## The Book of I John

JOHN, WHO HAD BEEN SO CLOSE TO JESUS IN EARLIER YEARS, WAS NOW THE LEADER OF THE CHRISTIANS AROUND EPHESUS.

"I have been with Jesus," John wrote to his people, "and I want you to have the same joy in knowing Him that I have. Don't believe anyone who says that God's Son did not come to the world as a real Person. God loved us and sent His Son to be our Savior. As He loved us, we should love one another."

## The Book of II John

"I was very glad," John wrote, "to find some of your children living by the truth and obeying God's command to love one another. If any enemies of the truth come to you teaching that Christ was not a real man, do not receive them into your house. If you do, you will be helping in this evil work."

## The Book of III John

"Dear Gaius," John wrote to his Christian friend, "I have heard good things about you. You are doing right in receiving Christians into your home, especially traveling preachers. Your kindness helps in their work. Don't pay attention to anyone who tries to stop you from doing this."

## The Book of Jude

JUDE, ANOTHER BROTHER OF JESUS, DID NOT BELIEVE THAT JESUS WAS THE SON OF GOD -- UNTIL HE ROSE FROM THE DEAD. THEN JUDE BECAME A CHRISTIAN AND AFTER THAT HE WAS A STRONG WORKER FOR CHRIST.
ONE DAY HE RECEIVED BAD NEWS -- THAT MEN IN SOME OF THE CHURCHES WERE TEACHING THINGS THAT WERE NOT TRUE.

JUDE WROTE THE CHURCHES A LETTER:

"*You must defend our Christian faith. You have been warned that people would try to turn you away from Christ. I understand some of these false teachers are with you now. Pray that God will keep you strong, and that He will help you strengthen others.*"

## The Book of Revelation

JOHN, WHO WROTE THE BEST-LOVED GOSPEL AND THREE LETTERS TO THE FOLLOWERS OF JESUS, ALSO WROTE THE BOOK OF REVELATION -- TO HELP CHRISTIANS FACE THE ANGRY POWER OF ROME.

THE ROMANS HAD ARRESTED JOHN AND SENT HIM AS A PRISONER TO THE ISLAND OF PATMOS. THERE HE SAW A VISION OF HEAVEN, AND HE HEARD JESUS SAY:

"BEHOLD, I STAND AT THE DOOR, AND KNOCK: IF ANY MAN HEAR MY VOICE, AND OPEN THE DOOR, I WILL COME IN TO HIM."

IN HEAVEN JOHN SAW THE BOOK OF LIFE -- IN WHICH WERE WRITTEN THE NAMES OF THOSE WHO LOVE CHRIST. AND FINALLY, THE OLD DISCIPLE SAW THE HOLY CITY, WHERE THERE IS NO SICKNESS, NO SORROW, NO DEATH. THOSE WHOSE NAMES ARE IN THE BOOK OF LIFE WILL ENTER THE GLORIOUS CITY AND LIVE FOREVER WITH CHRIST!

AND WITH JOHN'S VISION ENDS THE GREATEST STORY EVER TOLD, THE STORY OF THE BIBLE.

# How you can become part of God's wonderful family.

God loves families. After God made this world He created the first family, a man and a woman. Their names were Adam and Eve. Their first home was in the Garden of Eden, a place of wonderful living.

God is a good God, and He wanted only good things to happen to Adam and Eve. God told them what they should and should not do. Adam and Eve had the power to choose to obey God or to disobey Him.

Satan hated God. Satan came into the garden home of Adam and Eve disguised in the body of a snake. Satan told Eve that God had not told them the truth, and Eve believed what Satan was saying about the fruit. Adam knew he should not taste it, but he made a decision to disobey.

When Adam and Eve disobeyed God, something terrible happened. They became afraid and tried to hide from God. God told them that they had sinned and must leave the Garden of Eden. Instead of being a happy world, the earth became a sad place. Instead of love, there was hate, and people even began killing each other.

Cain and Abel were two sons of Adam and Eve. God told them that if they wanted their sins forgiven, they had to offer a perfect animal, one with absolutely nothing wrong with it, as sacrifice. Cain grew wonderful fruit and offered that to God, but God was displeased because Cain hadn't obeyed the instructions. Cain became jealous that God accepted the sacrifice of his brother but had rejected his, and so he became angry and killed Abel.

People continued to do evil and finally the world was so disobedient that God decided to destroy the world except for one man's family. That man, Noah, loved God and tried to obey God. So when God told him to build a huge boat, Noah did and was saved when the flood came.

For hundreds of years people who loved God obeyed him by sacrificing an animal to have their sins forgiven. Most of the world did not obey God, though, and worshiped gods they made with their own hands, gods made out of metal and wood.

A man named Abraham and his wife Sarah truly loved God. They had never had any children, which in those days was looked upon as a terrible problem. God said that even though they were old—over ninety years old—He would still give them a son and that the children of this son Isaac would became a famous nation.

Abraham loved Isaac, but one day God decided to test Abraham's faith, to see if God was first in his life. God asked Abraham to offer his son on an altar. Abraham had so much faith in God that he was willing to obey, but then God stopped him and told Abraham to offer an animal instead. Two thousand years later Jesus, God's only son, was crucified on that very same spot.

IF GOD WANTS ME TO GIVE HIM MY ONLY SON, I WILL OBEY.

When Canaan suffered a famine, Abraham's great-grandchildren moved to Egypt, where the Hebrews lived for 400 years. When the Egyptians turned against them and forced them to work as slaves, the people cried to God for help. He heard them and sent Moses to lead them from slavery.

Moses was saved as a baby when he was discovered by an Egyptian princess while being hidden in a floating basket. Many years later God called Moses from a burning bush and sent him to the Pharaoh. What followed was a contest of power and will between the Pharaoh and God.

245

The next morning the Pharaoh allowed the Hebrews to leave. Then later, he changed his mind again and sent his army after Moses and the people.

The Hebrews were trapped between the Egyptian army and the Red Sea. Then, in an awesome event which would bring praise to God for thousands of years, the sea opened and the Hebrews passed through on dry ground.

This event is known as the Exodus. The Passover Feast and the Exodus are examples of how God protects His family. These events are also symbols of how God makes a way for each person to escape from the slavery of sin and become part of His family.

Fifteen hundred years later, Jesus celebrated the Passover Feast each year, and it was at this feast just before He was killed that he conducted the famous "Last Supper" with his disciples.

After the Exodus, God called Moses to the top of Mount Sinai and gave him the Ten Commandments. These are God's instructions how people should live, and they are a measuring stick so people can see that they can't possibly live up to God's high standards. Everybody has broken at least one of these commandments. God calls breaking these commandments "sin."

I AM JEHOVAH YOUR GOD . . . YOU MAY WORSHIP NO OTHER GOD THAN ME.

YOU SHALL NOT MAKE YOURSELF ANY IDOLS.

YOU SHALL NOT USE THE NAME OF JEHOVAH YOUR GOD IRREVERENTLY.

OBSERVE THE SABBATH AS A HOLY DAY.

HONOR YOUR FATHER AND MOTHER.

YOU MUST NOT MURDER.

YOU MUST NOT COMMIT ADULTERY.

YOU MUST NOT STEAL.

YOU MUST NOT LIE.

YOU MUST NOT BE ENVIOUS OF YOUR NEIGHBOR'S HOUSE OR ANYTHING ELSE HE HAS.

GOD ALSO WISHED TO ESTABLISH A PLACE WHERE HIS PEOPLE COULD WORSHIP HIM. THE ISRAELITES FOLLOW HIS COMMANDS EXACTLY AND BUILD A HOUSE OF GOD CALLED "THE TABERNACLE." THE TABERNACLE WAS CONSTRUCTED BY EXPERT WEAVERS, AND THE FURNISHINGS WERE MADE OF GOLD, SILVER AND BRONZE BY MASTER CRAFTSMEN. THE TABERNACLE HAS A SPECIAL ROOM IN IT WHERE ONLY THE HIGH PRIEST CAN VISIT ONCE A YEAR. THIS SPECIAL ROOM IS CALLED "THE HOLY OF THE HOLIES" AND WAS WERE GOD MADE HIS PRESENCE KNOWN.

EVERY TIME THE NATION MOVED, THE PRIESTS PACKED UP THE TABERNACLE AND ALL ITS FURNISHINGS.

LOOK! MY ARM'S HEALED! I'M NOT GOING TO DIE!

NEITHER AM I!

Despite what God was constantly doing for His people, they would complain and disobey God. One day the Lord sent poisonous snakes among them to punish them, and many people were bitten and died.

Then the people asked for forgiveness for their sins, and the Lord told Moses, "Make a bronze replica of one of these snakes and attach it to the top of a pole. Anyone who is bitten shall live if he simply looks at it." This story is told as an example of how faith can save people from their sins.

Many times the people of Israel would worship the gods of the nations around them or forget to obey the instructions for following the true God. Then they would repent and ask God for forgiveness. The sacrifice of a perfect animal was always the way people could have their sins forgiven and come back to a good relationship with God.

Many years later King David's son Solomon was commissioned by God to build a wonderful permanent home for God called the Temple. At the Temple, sacrifices would be offered to God every day so that the people would be forgiven their sins. Although the Temple would be destroyed and rebuilt several times, it was the place where Jesus would visit and worship His Father.

In the 1000 years between King David and Jesus, the people of Israel often disobeyed God. For years, God's prophets asked the people to quit sinning and turn back to God. They also kept predicting that God would come as "The Messiah."

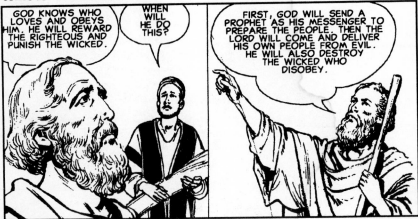

GOD KNOWS WHO LOVES AND OBEYS HIM. HE WILL REWARD THE RIGHTEOUS AND PUNISH THE WICKED.

WHEN WILL HE DO THIS?

FIRST, GOD WILL SEND A PROPHET AS HIS MESSENGER TO PREPARE THE PEOPLE. THEN THE LORD WILL COME AND DELIVER HIS OWN PEOPLE FROM EVIL. HE WILL ALSO DESTROY THE WICKED WHO DISOBEY.

The people of Israel were like all of us, because we have all done wrong. These wrong deeds and thoughts are called sins. The Bible says that everyone has rebelled against God and has lived sinfully. Our sins keep us from being part of God's family.

But God wants us to be part of His family. On our own, we could never earn a place in God's family—no matter how hard we try. But because God loves us so much and wants us to be close to Him, He had a special plan. God decided to become part of the human race. His Son, Jesus, would be born as a human baby, but without a human father.

One day, the Angel Gabriel came to a young unmarried girl named Mary, who was engaged to Joseph, a carpenter in Nazareth. The angel told her that her baby, born without a human father, would be totally holy—without sin. Many events at the beginning of Jesus' life confirmed what the angel told Mary.

Jesus lived a sinless life for 33 years. For the last three years he ministered to people around the country, telling them about God His Father, showing people how they should live, and displaying the power of God to do great miracles and to forgive sins.

The night before Jesus was arrested he celebrated the Feast of Passover with His disciples. The meal, eaten in an upper room, followed a 1,400 year tradition started by Moses. But then Jesus began a new tradition when he explained once more that he would give up His life to take away the sins of the world. Jesus used the bread and the wine as an example of His sacrifice. He once more explained God's plan for Him to die on the cross to take the punishment for all the wrongs that people everywhere have done.

Jesus not only predicted his death, but he also predicted that He would be brought back from the dead. He assured the disciples, "After I have been brought back to life again I will go to Galilee, and meet you there." Jesus added, "Everything written about me by the prophets will come true."

Shortly after that, Jesus was arrested. The Jesus who stilled the storm and raised Lazarus from the dead and fed 5,000 hungry people could have stopped the soldiers from arresting Him, from beating Him, and from nailing Him on the cross. But Jesus allowed himself to be killed because He was taking our punishment.

At the trial, Pilate declared that Jesus had done no wrong, but to please the crowd he sentenced Jesus to die on a cross.

When Jesus died, he was buried in a nearby tomb. It was sealed by a huge stone and guarded by soldiers because the leaders who put Him to death remembered what Jesus had said about coming back to life. But on the morning of the third day, a Sunday, a small group of women went to the tomb. Suddenly there was a great earthquake, and an angel of the Lord rolled aside the stone. The angel told the women, "Don't be frightened! . . . He isn't here, for He has come back to life again, just as He said He would. Come in and see where His body was lying . . . . And now go quickly and tell His disciples that He has risen from the dead, and that He is going to Galilee to meet them there."

To receive Jesus' payment for sin, you must make up your own mind to believe in Him. If we openly declare that Jesus died to forgive our sins, and believe that God raised Him from the dead, God promises to forgive and forget our sins. When we do this, we become members of God's family. The Holy Spirit comes to live in us and gives us the ability to live a Christian life. One day, we will go to Heaven to be with God forever.

Perhaps you've never made a conscious decision to confess your sin, ask God for His forgiveness, and live your life to honor Him. Why not pray this prayer now?

**Jesus, I believe that you are the Son of God.**

**I believe that you came to the earth to pay for our sins, including my sins.**

**I believe that you died and rose again, and that you are alive today.**

**Jesus, I ask you to forgive my sins, and make me a part of your wonderful family.**

**I ask you to come and live inside of me, and be my Lord.**

**Amen.**

I do believe! I have asked Jesus to become my Savior.

_____
(Name)                    (Date)

Here are some verses that should help you understand the decision you are making.

> John 3:16
>
> 1 John 5:11, 12
>
> John 1:12
>
> Romans 3:23
>
> Romans 5:8
>
> Romans 6:23
>
> Romans 10:9, 10
>
> 2 Corinthians 5:17

After you accept Christ's gift of salvation, read the Bible and talk with God in prayer. Soon, you will grow closer to Him and begin to enjoy the full life He intended as a member of God's wonderful family.

YES, IT WAS WRITTEN LONG AGO THAT THE MESSIAH MUST SUFFER AND DIE AND RISE AGAIN FROM THE DEAD ON THE THIRD DAY, AND THAT THIS MESSAGE OF SALVATION SHOULD BE TAKEN FROM JERUSALEM TO ALL THE NATIONS. THERE IS FORGIVENESS OF SINS FOR ALL WHO TURN TO ME. YOU HAVE SEEN THESE PROPHECIES COME TRUE.